TESTIMONIALS

"Rachel's story is a profound look into the world of someone who has risen from the depths of trauma to heal others on her journey to wellness. It is a story that will resonate with anyone who yearns to find meaning and lessons in life's challenges. In sharing the lessons she's learned, Rachel helps the reader uncover and transform their own trauma into a healing opportunity. I would highly recommend this book to anyone interested in personal transformation from someone who's taken the journey herself. To alchemize pain into growth is no small feat and one that can inspire us all."

– Carissa K.

"Rachel invites you into the most intimate moments of her life as she shares experiences that shaped her quest for self love, strength, and acceptance. From a young age, she knew she was meant for big things and didn't let challenges stop her on that journey. Instead, she forged on, learning coping mechanisms to heal her wounds, adapting to her ever-changing environment and became her authentic self. She is now offering up that spiritual and personal knowledge in this book. From the clever chapter names, to the reflection questions and list of resources, it's *apparent that Rachel is passionate about using what she has learned to help inspire others to do the same. Thank you Rachel for sharing your story and your passion. You've inspired me on a journey of self love and have given me tools I need to get started."*

– Jaime N.

"There are sometimes no words to describe the pain we have been through. A beautiful and powerful story of hope and transformation. Well done."

– Sarah N.

"I Sang Anyway tells Rachel's unique story and accomplishes what the memoir genre is so good at: connecting people across differing experiences to feel seen, to feel they are not alone. Rachel takes this work a step further by asking the reader to reflect upon their own individual experience. Healing is a long journey, and while our own traumas or life may differ greatly from hers, she invites us towards our own growth with the chapter-end reflection and exercises. Rachel's is a remarkable story, at once very specific to her and also universal in so many ways. The strength that is gained in making her voice heard, both I imagine for the author and also the reader, is uplifting in a way that left me thinking about it long after finishing the work. It is not a Pollyanna outlook on hard times, but instead an honest story of struggle and development, and in that is real hope. We are better for the shared voice and stories that are found here."

– Mia P.

"Rachel's remembrances are a combination of painful and compelling for those empathetic, somehow metamorphosed into a master class in how to avoid the pitfalls of bitterness and a desire for retribution. Neither of these powerhouse emotions serve us well, but dodging them takes maturity and a willingness to self-evaluate and set a different course toward releasing the negative experiences of the past and embracing positives in our lives.

In this memoir, Rachel not only found a mechanism to further her healing, she forged a pathway others may wish to follow, articulating points for the reader to absorb, ponder, and inspire.

Enduring, self-reflecting, and writing out her experiences and subsequent choices wasn't an easy task for her and compartmentalizing and overcoming the past won't be an easy task for anyone. We must remember that each new step forward on a journey toward a goal reinforces the worthiness of the healing choice."

– Nelle D.

"I Sang Anyway is a beautifully written book that helped me to better understand myself, my actions, my past, my present, and how to have a better future. The 'Questions for Reflection' led me to look at why I feel guilty or unworthy and gave me strategies to release myself from the guilt and enjoy the journey. As I read about Rachel's experiences, I thought about the little girl that I used to be, the mistakes that I made as a parent, and all the choices that led me to where I am today. I can't change the past, but I can heal myself and move forward from where I am. I believe this book is a gift to anyone who wants to free themselves from negative feelings and is open to truly looking within. Thank you, Rachel, for being brave enough to share your story so openly and honestly and create this wonderful book."

– Caroline K.

"You need to read this memoir! Bear witness to Rachel's personal life story and experience an empowering reminder to begin or continue your own path to healing. The thread of spiritual awakening and growth are inspiring for anyone, regardless of where they lie on their journey to self-fulfillment. Rachel's reconnection to her true self is a testament for anyone seeking their own truth. As much as it is deeply personal about Rachel, there is a familiarity of her tone that made me feel like she was right there next to me, telling me her life story. This story will help you know you are not alone, but recognized; and, further, empowered."

– Chantel H.

I Sang Anyway

I Sang Anyway

A Stepmom's Spiritual Memoir of Healing

RACHEL MERRILL

ACADEMY
PRESS

For permission requests, write to the below address:

Rachel Merrill
PYP Academy Press
141 Weston Street, #155
Hartford, CT, 06141

The opinions expressed by the author are not necessarily those held by PYP Academy Press.

Ordering Information: Quantity sales and special discounts are available on quantity purchases by corporations, associations, and others. For details, contact the author at the address above.

Edited by: Gail Marlene Schwartz and Nancy Graham-Tillman
Proofread by: Chloë Siennah
Cover design by: Nelly Murariu
Cover photo by: June Pearl Photography
Typeset by: Medlar Publishing Solutions Pvt Ltd., India

Printed in the United States of America.
ISBN: 978-1-955985-10-9 (hardcover)
ISBN: 978-1-955985-08-6 (paperback)
ISBN: 978-1-955985-09-3 (ebook)

Library of Congress Control Number: 2021918295

First edition, December 2021

The mission of the Publish Your Purpose Academy Press is to discover and publish authors who are striving to make a difference in the world. We give underrepresented voices power and a stage to share their stories, speak their truth, and impact their communities. Do you have a book idea you would like us to consider publishing? Please visit PublishYourPurposePress.com for more information.

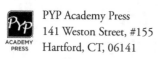 PYP Academy Press
141 Weston Street, #155
Hartford, CT, 06141

DEDICATION

Dedicated to
my son, my shining star.

CONTENTS

Foreword . . . . *xvii*

Letter to the Reader . . . . *xix*

Introduction . . . . *xxi*

PART ONE: Soul Cry

CHAPTER 1: Prelude 3
Ora et Labora

CHAPTER 2: Accompaniment 11
Ancestry

CHAPTER 3: Piano 13
Lost Voice

CHAPTER 4: Baritone 19
Different Faces of Dad

CHAPTER 5: Aria 21
Writing a New Reality

CHAPTER 6:   Dolente 25
     Bullied at School

CHAPTER 7:   Pianissimo 29
     Abused

CHAPTER 8:   Cymbals 35
     Revealing the Abuse at Church

CHAPTER 9:   Largo 39
     Late Bloom

CHAPTER 10: Minor Key 43
     #metoo

CHAPTER 11: Accelerando 51
     My Uncle's Arrest

CHAPTER 12: Syncopation 53
     Dreams

CHAPTER 13: Sforzando 55
     Engaged

CHAPTER 14: Lullaby 59
     My Son, My Greatest Joy

CHAPTER 15: A Cappella 61
     Homeless

CHAPTER 16: Trill 65
     Living in Poverty

CHAPTER 17: Tutti 69
     Find Your People

CHAPTER 18: Dirge 73
     Trisha

CHAPTER 19: Duet 79
     Conan

PART TWO: Soul Roar

CHAPTER 20: Coda 85
Divorce

CHAPTER 21: Impressionism 87
Proposal

CHAPTER 22: Violin 89
The Baby that Could Have Been

CHAPTER 23: Serenade 91
My Stepdaughter, Born Through My Heart

CHAPTER 24: Ensemble 95
Family Reunion

CHAPTER 25: Forte 99
Triggered by Dad

CHAPTER 26: Shrill 101
Bitter Valentine

CHAPTER 27: Crescendo 105
Meeting for Coffee

CHAPTER 28: Staccato 109
Black Lives Matter

CHAPTER 29: Fortissimo 115
It Gets Worse

CHAPTER 30: Glissando 127
The Eating Disorder

PART THREE: Soul Song

CHAPTER 31: Home Key 135
Full Custody of Ginger

CHAPTER 32: Harmony. 139
  It Is Safe to Be Me

CONCLUSION: Outro 143
  A New Dawn

Aknowledgments. *151*
Appendix: Legato *153*
About the Author *157*

FOREWORD

By Iman Gatti

I have adored Rachel from our very first meeting, many years ago, while she was a student in an online program where I was a guest speaker.

It did not take long for me to understand how truly gifted and loving Rachel is. She has this gentle yet powerful and enriching, healing energy. Her presence is calming and puts you at ease, and her vulnerability shows you her immense strength of character and capacity for love.

I had the pleasure of working with Rachel as she was committing to write this incredible book that you are about to read.

I was so touched when she asked me to write her foreword. What a deep and meaningful honour it is to be part of such lovely work as *I Sang Anyway*. Even the title moved me, as I know personally just how magical Rachel's actual singing voice is! She is a woman filled with song and poetry.

Throughout these pages lie an extraordinary testament to one woman's ability to not only withstand soul crushing pain, but to become a woman who has this immeasurable capacity for love and healing.

I Sang Anyway is a heartfelt invitation to find a place within yourself to listen to your inner voice, so that you may also powerfully heal and show up in your life and share your own gifts.

I am so very proud of Rachel for making this dream come true and for her commitment to knowing herself and sharing her voice with the world. It is a deep privilege to call her my student and friend.

May her words guide you and call you back to yourself, may these pages bring you the miracle of healing, forgiveness, and hope, and may you always have the courage to sing your own song.

Big Juicy Love,

Iman
Best Selling Author, Coach, and Speaker
www.ImanGatti.com

LETTER TO
THE READER

D ear Reader,
You are a healing warrior.

This memoir was written to inspire you to share your truth and provide healing wisdom you can put to practical use. At the end of each chapter, you will find spiritual tools and reflection questions to help you along your own healing journey, whether you are at the beginning of or farther down your path. These reflection questions may be useful for journaling, or you can use them with a women's group or book club.

While I wrote my story from my perspective, I honor that others may view what happened differently. As much as possible, I have tried to protect identities by changing names of the people and places in this book with the exception of spiritual healers who have given me permission to use their names. Some of the characters may share traits of combinations of real people, and some physical descriptions have been changed. All of this is to respect their privacy while sharing my authentic truth.

I am honored that you chose this book, at this time. May you find comfort in these pages and through your own search for peace. You are more powerful than you know.

With love,

Rachel Merrill

Rachel

INTRODUCTION

As a little girl, I fervently believed that one day I would become a pop star. With every movie and novel that I consumed, my heart sparkled with the idea that I, too, could become the adored diva of my dreams. At a diner near my college, I remember telling a friend very seriously that one day I would be a famous singer.

Although I didn't create the pop star career I longed for, after a lifetime of suffering in silence as a survivor of childhood domestic violence, adult sexual assault, and my husband's high-conflict ex-wife, I found my voice with the help of professionals and used it to heal myself. I found my boundaries and my inner calm. I began to choose myself and trust my intuition. As a result of my spiritual awakening, I am finally reclaiming my voice and am at peace with who I am: a bisexual, witchy woman now owning her truth after hiding for so long. I am free.

Perhaps as you read these words, you are suffering. Maybe, like me, your suffering is from abuse. Or maybe your suffering is from something else. Maybe my words resonate with you, and your suffering is why you chose to read this book. Your frustration may be causing you to look for relief. I am living proof that healing is possible and that you, too, can heal by applying the wisdom from this book.

Woven throughout my own story, you will find spiritual wisdom and sparks of inspiration to forge your own healing path and find your own voice. You will benefit from my years of reading spiritual books, my paying for and teaching spiritual courses, my experience becoming a Reiki Master, my reconnection to nature, my love of music, and more. You will learn how to hear your innermost voice and how to use it as the compass for your life.

In several chapters of my memoir, I refer to Indigenous people of the Americas. I want to be clear that I am wary of cultural appropriation and appropriating anything is never my intent. When referencing Native American rituals, I consulted with a Diné (Navajo) medicine woman named Jeanita Kennedy and asked for her permission. I offer these descriptions with humble reverence and respect for Indigenous peoples and their traditions and rituals.

Since I was 12, I yearned to share my voice on stage. After experiencing the COVID-19 pandemic and the devastation my family faced in 2020, I finally decided my voice and my story could wait no longer. Now as I share my memoir, I encourage you to visit my website, www.rachelmerrill.me, to begin or continue your healing journey and allow your inner voice to come forth. Whether you believe in God or not, honoring your inner voice will help you create the life you have always wanted to live. And when you begin to speak your truth, a new dawn begins.

"For us, warriors are not what you think of as warriors.
The warrior is not someone who fights, because no one has the right to
take another life. The warrior, for us, is one who sacrifices himself for
the good of others. His task is to take care of the elderly, the defenseless,
those who cannot provide for themselves, and above all, the children,
the future of humanity."

– Sitting Bull

PART ONE

SOUL CRY

Lost Voice

CHAPTER ONE

PRELUDE

Prelude: *(genre) 1) a free-form introductory movement to a fugue or other more complex composition; 2) a term used instead of overture (by Wagner, Bizet, and other later Romantic composers) to show dramatic unity between the introductory orchestral music and the theatrical drama that follows it*

Some would say I should have died.
Nearly drowning in a pool, almost being hit by a train, and undergoing emergency surgery didn't kill me. My father almost did.
Decades later, my stepdaughter's mother nearly strangled the life out of her.
My stepdaughter and I are still here, and I am ready to speak my truth.
This is my memoir.

At the beginning of 2020, a medium told me that to achieve greater healing I needed to go back to my family's Deerpath Farm in North Dakota and perform a ritual on the earth. I planned to buy a plane ticket there from my current home on the East Coast, yet a week later the United States was under quarantine due to COVID-19. I canceled my travel plans and began to wonder how I would go back to my roots. How would I achieve this great healing that my soul cried out for? I thought I had slammed shut the North Dakota chapter of my book because it had brought me so much pain. Yet my deeply sad childhood haunted me. I decided that while I could not physically travel to the vast prairie, I could journey there in spirit with this book. I decided that this book would bring me the healing for which I would give anything. This book is my healing ritual.

A STORMY START

Just four days before my birth, a winter storm that started as rain and sleet and turned into ten inches of snow over the course of two days hit the Zeeland, North Dakota area. In the aftermath of the storm, on their one-year wedding anniversary, my parents sped their white 1980 Chevy Citation to the Zeeland hospital. It was November 22nd, 1981. In the bitter cold of a November morning, after a snowstorm blanketed the frosted fields, I was born their first child. My hair and eyes were dark like my father's; and so, I was named after the man who would teach me a lesson that would take half my lifetime to learn: we read the sheet music of life very differently.

When my parents brought me home from the hospital, they drove east from Zeeland on the two-lane highway, passed brown and snow-covered fields and abandoned farmhouses, rose seven miles onto a gravel road that dipped down a hill, and turned slightly to the south toward the Deerpath Farm. The gravel driveway was a quarter mile long, flat, and went straight past large wheat, corn, and sunflower fields and rows of elm trees. The trees were strategically placed in rows to protect the soil and to shield our farmhouse.

The prairie was vast and I could see for many miles because the land has more cows, wheat fields, and bison than people. The wind was constant and during the coldest of days, my nose hairs felt stiff and I could feel my lungs begin to harden. The land held a stark beauty that felt dotted with questions of the past. What happened in the days of cowboys and Native Americans? What happened 100 years ago? What is this place that on the surface looks peaceful, but if you stop to listen with your heart, you can feel its tumult?

North Dakota is in the geographic center of North America. The state was one of the last states to become part of the United States. Previously, it had "belonged" to France and was part of the Louisiana Purchase. North Dakota was really the frontier of the "Wild West." The Mandan, Hidatsa, Arikara, Sioux (Dakota and Lakota, meaning friends or allies), and Chippewa people were among the original people to live on the land before German, Dutch, Norwegian, and other settlers arrived due to the Free Land Act of 1865. This act happened the same year that slavery ended in the United States. My paternal Dutch ancestors were among the settlers who chose North Dakota as their home.

I remember the first time I discovered a Native American artifact in my family's garden on our farm near Zeeland, North Dakota. I was a child, perhaps eight years old, digging in the dirt with my hands to avoid actually weeding. "What's this?" I asked my mother. "Oh, that's an arrowhead," she responded nonchalantly, as if every garden has arrowheads in them. No one had mentioned a word about the stone circles out on the prairie or the other items that had been found in the earth decades and even a century ago as a result of the Native Americans being pushed onto the Standing Rock Reservation on the western side of the Missouri River. No one told me that my own great-uncle had self-published a book in which he referred to Native Americans as "savages."

ORA ET LABORA

When my paternal ancestors came to this land in 1886, they built a sod house and began farming. In 1903, they built the family homestead that first my great-grandfather lived in, then my grandfather after that, then my father, and then me. I was born exactly one year to the day after my parents married in 1980 and was named after my dad. Both facts are ironic to me because I know that my mother didn't want my birthday to be the same day as their anniversary, and I am named after the very person who brought me great suffering.

Although I don't know much about my maternal ancestors, I know that my maternal grandmother was a nurse who assisted Dr. Michael DeBakey, a pioneer of open-heart surgery in Texas. My paternal grandmother was a "Rosie the Riveter" during World War II in Chicago. I like to think that coming from this line of women meant that it was always written in the stars for me to be a healing warrior.

On the outside of my house, above the windows of my blue bedroom, was a rainbow-shaped sign. On the left side of the arch it said 1886, and on the right side it said 1903. In the middle were the Latin words *Ora et Labora*, which translates to "Pray and Work." These words described my parents perfectly. My mom was consumed with praying and my dad was consumed with working. She was the Pray; he was the Work.

My mother, Debbie, grew up as a pastor's kid in upstate New York, Iowa, and Ohio and settled in the Chicago, Illinois area with her brother and parents when she was a teenager. She was a city girl who never planned to stay in North Dakota past her first year of teaching; that is, until she met my dad. She was a cheerful, smiling woman with a generous heart and an eye for pies. She loved eating and describing foods, especially double-fudge brownies, rhubarb and cherry pies, and Bundt cakes. One of her favorite things was buying presents for her family and friends. Her movements were quick and completed nervously. Debbie's blue eyes, short and permed blonde hair, large-framed glasses, and professional piano training made her the perfect person to play the organ at Dutch Reformed Christian Church on Sundays and the piano as the music teacher in elementary school. Debbie enjoyed wearing long skirts or green pants and long earrings or necklaces. She never complained and instead recited Bible verses. As a child, she paid me to memorize Bible verses. Each morning, she could be found reading her Bible with her devotion book and then in prayer. We were Calvinists who believed in predestination (aka you are born with God already deciding whether you are going to heaven or hell).

My mother raised us to be a very musical family. I sang at church, learned to play the piano some, and for eight years played the alto saxophone. In school, I was in choir and band. I competed in and won some state competitions for singing and playing saxophone.

My father, Ryan, grew up in the house where I did, absorbing the painful energy of the Native American bones crying out from the ground. I may never know exactly how he became so angry, sad, and depressed, but knowing the history of the land in North Dakota left me believing that the sadness of those Native bones lived in him. He was not Native American; in fact, he was of Dutch ancestry. Being around him was like entering a cloud of cigarette smoke where an explosion was waiting to happen. This was not the smoke of a peace pipe by any means. My dad had a darkness about him that I could feel whether my eyes were open or closed. His dark brown eyes were heavy and often stormy under his thick black eyebrows. His dark hair covered his forehead and matched the mustache above his standard frown. Surprisingly, this version of the man that I saw on a regular basis was not generally seen by people in town. In public, he was a member of a social club and a leader in our church. I was told Ryan was the life of the party growing up; in town he was quite popular. Back at home, while this side of him occasionally peered into our house, we generally knew that his words reverberated with inflexible resolve. What he said was final.

Although I was often afraid of my dad, I was not afraid of him when he sang. He had the most marvelously deep voice that soared over other men's voices in church. When he was in a good mood, he would often sing songs from the 1960s, '70s, and '80s.

As the third-generation farmer to live in our homestead, my father carried the pressure of maintaining the family farm. He had, in fact, left college to help my grandfather with the farm when my grandfather was sick. I sometimes wondered what the environment of the farm had been like for him growing up, since he carried an anger, and it seemed that my uncle did too. One of my aunts married a man who could be quite angry. And my other aunt was very quiet. I pondered what must have happened to them, which was strange because all I knew of my grandparents was that they were so loving and kind to me.

Another factor influencing my father was our Christian religion. The way that my parents believed in Christianity was to put God first, then men, then women, then children—in that order. Women were to listen to men without exception, and so forth.

SIBLINGS

When my sister Josephine ("Josie") was born, I was all of 16 months old. She came into this world nearly albino white, with silvery blonde hair and bright blue eyes. Unlike my hair, hers grew out stick-straight to frame her face. Because of our nearness in age and her quick smile, we instantly grew close. Josie grew up to play the clarinet, piano, and other instruments, then became a music and piano teacher like our mother.

In 1985, my sister, Sophie, was born with hazel eyes and dark blonde hair. Her chameleon eyes were like her mood, changing depending on the aching way that my father stormed into the house. Sophie played the flute at first, but then decided to become a cheerleader in high school. Finally, in 1990, my brother, Brandon, was born with the bluest eyes, chubby cheeks, and blonde hair. I called him "cutie" for many more years than he enjoyed. I loved pinching his cheeks and playing with him like a little doll. Brandon played the drums until he decided to play football instead.

While my father often took his rage out on us girls, I was most often the target. I remember being a happy, bubbly, popular child until the summer after kindergarten.

I can only imagine the stress of having three young girls born so close together and overseeing a family farm that stretched for 2,000 acres. What my father didn't seem to reflect on was that each time he stormed into our home fresh from helping the cows with calving or from baling the hay, we three small girls absorbed all his anger. We felt the deep, deep disappointment of our existence. When I complained to my mother about his emotional and sometimes physical abuse, she would say, "He is a stressed-out farmer." She excused our words away until we stopped saying anything about it at all.

HEALING WISDOM

Go to your roots to discover why you may be struggling to heal. If possible, touch the earth where you grew up. Ask your family questions. Discover where your suffering truly came from and why it happened.

QUESTIONS FOR REFLECTION

What is the lesson in your suffering? Who is to blame for your suffering? What would happen if you chose to see yourself with love, despite what happened to you?

Second baby from the left: Rachel, around 1982

CHAPTER TWO

ACCOMPANIMENT

Accompaniment: *a musical part that supports or partners a solo instrument, voice, or group*

ANCESTRY

Although my father was a difficult and angry man, I won the lottery with my aunts, uncles, cousins, grandparents, and extended family. These were and are, with few exceptions, the sweetest people. If you can imagine a family full of generous, happy, enthusiastic, helpful, lovely people, then you can imagine them. Although they may not take up as much space in my story, I want to be sure to point out that they all taught me about unconditional love. They were and *are* love. With most of this family, I am the luckiest. But I didn't always see it that way because I was so focused on how my father treated me.

We grew up very Dutch. My grandparents owned wooden shoes. During one Fourth of July parade in a tiny neighboring town, I was on a float with my great-aunt and great-uncle for our Dutch Reformed Church. I wore wooden shoes, a traditional blue and white dress, and a white hat that turned up on the ends. I sat on the back of a truck bed as we drove down the gravel road that was the main street of that tiny town. At one point, the pickup truck hit a bump and the Christian Reformed flag fell and hit me on the head! I laugh about it now, but I am sure I cried about it then. My great-aunt and great-uncle were there to comfort me.

Great-aunt Gertie was a small, joyful woman who was excited about life. She *was* joy. And her husband, Great-uncle Abe, balanced her with his serene calm and his steady, watchful gaze. He ensured all was well. By my own request, they both initiated me into the Reformed Church with catechism (Christian teaching) when I was 11. Although as an adult I do not follow the beliefs of Calvinism and predestination, I know they taught me from a place of love and generosity.

My grandfather grew up speaking only Dutch until he attended school where he learned English. I remember wearing a pin that said, "If you ain't Dutch, you ain't much!" I smile at the irony of international relations becoming an important focus of my career.

HEALING WISDOM

If I had learned to acknowledge my pain, let it go, and then focus on *gratitude* for all of the wonderful people in my life, I believe I would have been much happier. Find people you trust to mentor you and allow yourself to receive kindness from them. Gratitude is a magnet for joy.

QUESTIONS FOR REFLECTION

What did you have to be grateful for when you were growing up? Did you have anyone you could confide in? What about now? What top five people, places, or things are on your gratitude list?

CHAPTER THREE

PIANO

Piano: *(dynamic; p) a quiet dynamic marking*

LOST VOICE

A distinct memory comes to me as I close my eyes and the innocence of childhood comes flowing back to me. I see myself playing sweetly with my sisters Sophie and Josephine. We were so excited playing with our brand new 1980s Play-Doh Salon set with miniature bald people who could have Play-Doh "hair" pumped through their heads. We sat at the kitchen table, pumping the little people up on the miniature salon chair and cutting their Play-Doh hair with tiny plastic scissors. My sisters and I sometimes argued over who would get to create the next fabulous hairstyle, but we had so much fun!

When we were done playing with the mini bald people, we ran off to play with our little brother. I would like to think that we tidied up the table, but we most likely ran away from the table and left a large mess for my mother to clean.

Shortly after we left the room, we could hear my dad arriving at home. He was instantly yelling, "DEBBIE! I don't know how many times I need to tell you! Dinner needs to be on the table at 6:00 pm sharp! You think I have all night to wait around for my meal?!" I could hear things slamming in the other room. My sisters and I looked at each other with wide eyes. Cupboards were opening and banging shut.

"GIRLS!" We straightened up quickly to the sound of his voice. "Help your mother!" And he began to mutter something to himself as we scrambled to figure out what to do.

As I entered the kitchen, I could see my dad throwing something onto the floor. "NO ONE EVER PICKS ANYTHING UP AROUND HERE!" he yelled as he hurled a box to the floor and began stomping on it. He stomped and stomped, yelling as he jumped all over the box. Whatever was in the box was making a loud crunching noise as his steel-toed boots crushed it over and over again until everything inside was destroyed. My dad stormed outside to smoke a cigarette, and I peered nervously over at the box to see what it was. My heart sank as I saw with shock that it was the Play-Doh Salon set. How could he do this? It was our favorite toy. Tears began to stream down my face, but I quickly wiped them away before anyone could see that I was having emotions. I didn't want to get yelled at more for showing sadness.

Sophie started to cry loudly. "No, no, no!!! Not the Play-Doh set!!! Why???"

"SHUT UP!!! Just SHUT UP!" my dad was already back inside yelling. I felt sick listening to his voice. I was so sad, confused, and angry. Why did he hate us so much? He treated us girls so much worse than my brother, always yelling at us and making us feel terrible. I wished my mother would say something, but instead she looked down at the floor.

WALLFLOWER

When I went to church or anywhere in the community, if people said hi to me I barely smiled and didn't say hi back. I didn't see myself as worthy enough of their attention. I felt that because my dad discarded me, no one else would want me. And silence seemed like the best option. At that point, I preferred food over words crossing my lips. It seemed better to hide than to be myself.

In first grade, I started overeating to deal with my father's disapproval. I remember how I turned to food to soothe me when I stood at the brownie pan, eating more and more. I remember eating more than a serving of chips at once and taking more and more candy from the candy drawer. Over the summer between kindergarten and first grade, I had eaten my pain away. It felt so good to control my emotions through my lips.

My angels and guides had never given up on me, and they began giving me signs and pieces of wisdom from a young age. The first sign I remember was a poster of a sad-looking puppy hung up at my elementary school that said something along the lines of, "Sometimes people are waiting for you to be their friend first." This caused me to pause and think that perhaps others feel insecure like me. Perhaps they are nervous to form friendships and trust others too.

A memory burned in my mind is of my young, first-grade self talking to a boy named Lewis who was in the class above mine. We had played together and been close friends. When I allowed the sadness and pain to creep in about my father, I remember Lewis saying to me as I put my boots away from playing in the snow outside, "You used to be fun. I don't know what happened." And that young Rachel took this to heart, too, as another person's disapproval. I felt it in my soul.

As I grew older—I believe partly because I was born an old soul and partly because I am an empath—the serious side of me prayed fervently each day for wisdom for myself and blessings for others. I remember feeling my heart chakra being so big that the entire world was wrapped inside of my love. I loved everyone else so much and yet I didn't love myself. It was easier, in fact a simple distraction, to love others more. It made me feel better if I was giving to others and expecting nothing for myself. I lay in my bed at night, sometimes crying for the pain of the world. While this may have seemed like a noble and Jesus-like thing to do, I was ignoring my own feelings. I was unable to separate myself from others' pain and so it became mine too. This belief was toxic, yet I carried it with me for many years. Only in my late 20s did I start to realize that I was worthy of love.

At home, I never knew which version of my father I would experience from moment to moment. Sometimes he would sit calmly in his recliner with the *Bismarck Tribune* newspaper or watch a Rocky Balboa movie with quiet ease. Sometimes he would eat meat and potatoes calmly at the dinner table. But often he would be set off by the smallest, most unexpected things. He would fly into a rage without notice.

I decided that because each day felt like walking on eggshells, making jokes to cheer up my sisters would become my job. I was often blunt, and I loved to use candidly surprising humor to amuse my little sisters. I felt the most brave and bold when I was with them. I knew they didn't judge me for being myself. I felt free to be myself, even if my sense of humor was sometimes an irritation to them.

One evening at the dinner table in our eat-in kitchen, my dad seemed to have a cloud of darkness above his head. He was quiet and staring off at nowhere in particular with a frown on his tanned face as he chewed.

It was dessert time. We had dessert after nearly every dinner, and sometimes after lunch too. That evening's dessert was my grandmother's homemade fudge. My dad scooped up a large spoonful of fudge and positioned it near his lips.

I piped up with enthusiasm, "Have enough fudge there?" I thought I was hilarious. Perhaps we would create a close emotional bond through humor, I thought, feeling excited about this possibility.

My dad's spoon dropped to the table and his mustache bristled. He slammed his fist so hard down onto the table that it shook. I jumped in my seat. "GO TO YOUR ROOM!!!!!" he roared. My sisters and mom looked down at their plates quietly. No one said a word. Each time something like this happened, I felt a shock to my entire system. It was as if I was connected to jumper cables and his rage jolted me to my core.

We could hear our dog barking outside. My dad sneered, "I'm going to go outside and shoot that dog."

Gingerly, I rose from my seat as his angered gaze pierced through my flesh and into my heart. He looked at me with utter disdain and disgust. "GET OUT OF HERE NOW!!!" he screamed, enough to make the walls shake. I turned and scrambled to leave the kitchen and head to the stairs that led to my bedroom. I ran up the stairs with tears streaming down my face.

That night, I couldn't sleep. All I could see in my mind was my dad's infuriated face. I would have given anything for him to love me and treat me with respect. I snuck down the stairs to the kitchen where I found a bag of chips on the counter, picked it up, and headed back upstairs. Standing on the green carpet right outside of my bedroom, I set the bag of chips on the bookcase next to my bedroom door. It was about midnight. I reached into the bag and began pulling out handfuls of salty, delicious potato chips, cramming fistfuls of them past my lips and savoring each bite. I felt euphoric putting as much food into my mouth as possible and instantly felt so much pleasure from the flavor, the satisfying crunch, and the control. I could control my happiness at this moment. All thoughts of my father faded away as I ate golden chip after salty chip. All I could see was this beautiful, clear bag of chips that felt as though they nourished me where I did not otherwise feel nourished.

HEALING WISDOM

When I was so damaged, I wasn't very in touch with my feelings because it felt better to be numb. And so, I began my attempt at the healing process by trying to use my analytical mind to fix the problem. I went to counseling, took medication, and tried all the things that others said would fix me. I followed the instructions, tried the new diet, then created the new schedule. But no matter what I tried, the painful hole remained in my heart. Because I was using the mind to try to fix what can only be fixed with the heart. When I began to allow myself to *feel* all the pain and all the pleasure, that is when the healing truly began.

QUESTIONS FOR REFLECTION

When is a time that you found it easier to be numb than to feel the pain? What happened as a result of your numbness? What would you have said or done if you allowed yourself to feel pain and talked about it with someone?

CHAPTER FOUR

BARITONE

Baritone: *a moderately low male voice; in range between a tenor and a bass*

For my 11th or 12th birthday, my parents threw a birthday party for me in our church basement. My closest friends were there. We gathered around a table to wait for food. I was feeling down because I didn't know how my dad would treat my friends.

My dad suddenly came waltzing out of the kitchen and over to our table, holding a pizza on a tray. He beamed as he placed the pizza in front of us and started cracking jokes. My friends were laughing hysterically as I watched the scene with bewilderment. Everyone was so happy. I felt relieved and confused. I was thankful my dad was acting appropriately, but I wondered why he couldn't treat me this kindly when my friends weren't there to watch.

Around the same year, my dad's cousin, Jeremy, came to live with us and help my dad work on the farm for the better part of a year. Jeremy stayed in my room, and I shared my sister Josie's room. My sisters and I were enthralled with his dreadlocks and his stories of California. In fact, we had a picture of my sisters and I touching Jeremy's hair. I can still remember finding him as I was out for a walk; he was seated on the side of the gravel road, watching the sunset over the prairie. He told me that, without such wide-open spaces, you couldn't see a sunset like that in Los Angeles.

I only found out as an adult that Jeremy had been staying with us because my dad offered him a place to recover from some of his dangerous choices. My dad had offered Jeremy a safe harbor. This discovery revealed my dad's compassionate side—and it gave me a startling new perspective as an adult.

HEALING WISDOM

Get to the root of your thoughts. See where they grow. Are they growing into the sun and blossoming, or are they snarling down and becoming tangled in the weeds? By changing the course of your thoughts, you are opening a world of possibility. You become the alchemist.

QUESTIONS FOR REFLECTION

When someone does something that is hurtful to you, how can you stand up for yourself? What would happen if you asked them whether your perception of what they did was true? For example, "When you did this, I felt that you didn't care about me. Is that true?" Journal about what you might say next based on both a positive and negative reaction from the other person.

CHAPTER FIVE

ARIA

Aria: *a beautiful manner of solo singing, accompanied by orchestra, with a steady metrical beat*

When I was 12 years old, I prayed to God to make me into a published writer and a famous singer. On my bed covered in blue Care Bear sheets, I begged with an open heart, clasped hands over my chest, and a yearning so big that the boundless prairies of North Dakota could not contain it. I felt safe in two places: on stage, singing in front of a crowd, and anywhere with a pen, writing in the pages of my notebook as the author of my destiny. When I lived in these creative spaces, I felt free. I felt that Rachel became Rose: a blossoming, beautiful flower instead of the wallflower I saw myself as.

The heroine of my books was always named Rose. In the books I wrote beginning at age 12, I was Rose, and my friends Abby, Jamie, and Kristy each had their roles in my stories. Our adventures took us through the streets of Paris on the Champs Elysée, through the rolling vineyards of Italy, and past the skyscrapers of New York City. Wherever we were in my stories felt far more interesting to me than my family's farm or my tiny hometown.

Each time I became upset, I ate junk food and went to my room to write. I enjoyed controlling my pleasure through food. I wrote while sitting on my dark blue, well-worn armchair, staring out of my bedroom windows that overlooked our gravel driveway and the corral for our beef cattle. My chair was to the left of a bookshelf filled with my favorite books and porcelain dolls. In this chair, I created other worlds with my pen in hand.

I wrote whenever I could: on the bus to school, in school during study hall, and sometimes in my big, grassy backyard surrounded by elm trees, white spruce, and balsam firs. I wrote so often that I developed a callous on the middle finger of my left hand. The side of my hand was often smeared with blue or black ink. I plotted story twists and turns in my daydreams and sometimes pieces of my stories came to me in my sleep.

For my 13th birthday, I asked for a *Writer's Market* book filled with publisher information. For my 14th birthday, I attended International Music Camp for writing near the Peace Gardens along the North Dakota/Manitoba border. When I returned home, I remember excitedly sharing one of the stories I had written. I gave my notebook to my grandfather to read when I visited him. He read through part of the story and looked up at me from his Afghan-covered recliner in surprise. "When you write these stories, do you have an outline first? Or do you just write it?" "I just write it! I write it and keep creating it. I usually know what's next in my head."

The escape from reality was everything for me. I felt like I was truly in the flow until the pen stopped and I looked up. Until I had to see my dad. Until I had to wonder from one moment to the next whether he would hurl a barrage of hateful comments at me or leave me alone. I was deeply depressed with no concept of what depression was, knowing only that the escape in the pages of my novels was my favorite disappearing act. I hoped maybe one day I could disappear to another country, maybe by joining the Peace Corps.

WITCHES

When I was lonely in school, I would often find myself in the library. Because of my awkwardness, I found it easier to concentrate on pages than people. I loved to read for ideas and to experience more than the quiet streets of

Zeeland. While searching the bookshelves for something interesting, I found a book about the Salem Witch Trials that occurred from 1692–1693. With intrigue, I read the descriptions of the supposed convulsions of the women and viewed the terrible drawings. I wondered about these women, and something quietly stirred inside of me, wanting to know more. I slammed the book shut, determined to keep away from what looked terribly evil. I was raised to believe it was evil and had no idea that as I grew older, I would change my mind.

At home, I had a monthly book subscription for a little while and a library card. I read about how to summon fairies, life after death experiences, and what I now understand was shamanism. The Merriam-Webster dictionary defines shamanism as: "A religion practiced by Indigenous peoples of far northern Europe and Siberia that is characterized by belief in an unseen world of gods, demons, and ancestral spirits responsive only to the shamans." In my living room on the orange shag carpet, I practiced yoga with a Video Home System (VHS) tape, and I created a dream box where I placed special things inside such as candles, cut out magazine photos, and my written wishes. As an adult, I discovered that this kind of box is used by witches for spells. These were my first clues to revealing my true nature. On the outside, however, I fervently practiced Christianity.

ANGELS

The one place I didn't mind being seen by others was on stage singing. Although I felt awkward in my body, when I stepped in front of the microphone at church to sing, I felt my true self pouring forth. The shape of my body didn't matter to me when I sang. Instead, I felt truly free and truly seen. The beauty I felt on the inside was shared through my voice outside.

I often had solos at church, and my mom either played the piano or the electric organ to accompany me. My dad rarely complimented me, but when he did, it was about my singing. He said to my mom, "Her voice is smooth like butter. It's like Karen Carpenter." This praise made my heart glow more than any compliments from the congregation.

When I created my books and refined my singing, I felt that the creation was a direct connection to the Divine. This belief was confirmed after my mom and I listened to a cassette tape recording of my singing at church. "Oh my goodness!" she exclaimed. "It sounds like an angel is singing with you!"

And it was true. In perfect harmony, I could hear another voice joining mine. And no one had been singing with me. This was my first experience believing angels were with me.

HEALING WISDOM

Create what brings you joy. When I was depressed, the best way out of my depression was to turn anger into constructive action. Because what you focus on expands into your reality, focus on the reality you want to create.

QUESTIONS FOR REFLECTION

What are some behaviors you notice that distract you from your pain? If you were to replace one habit with a better one, what would it be? What are the excuses you tell yourself to prevent shifting your behavior?

CHAPTER SIX

DOLENTE

Dolente: *sorrowful, plaintive*

In high school, while most people were nice to me, some were awful. One afternoon, a boy mooed at me while his friends laughed as I passed by in the hall. I was a big girl, shaped rather like a football player, and with the added sensitivity of being an empath, the teasing truly stung. I felt everything magnified times ten.

When I started to become extra self-conscious from the teasing, I asked my mom to buy me some workout tapes. One was yoga, and one was Denise Austin. One morning as I was jumping around in the living room in front of the TV to Denise Austin's purple leotard exercises, my dad saw me working out. "Don't wear out the carpet!" he said. Maybe he was kidding, but it didn't really matter. I felt crushed.

The next morning, after a boy on the bus threw trash at the back of my head, I made my way to class and saw my crush, Miguel, leaving the room. I noticed which desk he had been at, and I decided to start leaving him notes written in pencil on the desk. I made the notes anonymous, and they said things like, "My favorite candy is Skittles. What's yours?"

Without knowing who I was, Miguel started to respond by leaving notes. We wrote notes back and forth on the desk several times before I worked up the courage to write him an anonymous note on a piece of paper. On the note, I told him that he could find out who I was if he went to the location of my locker and described my locker. My face flushed red as I thought of the possibility that maybe he liked me too.

Later, when class was over and I made my way down the one hallway in the high school, I stopped by my locker to gather my things. Miguel and a friend were watching me as I walked right up to the locker I had described in the note. I felt myself blushing as I imagined him coming to talk to me.

I put my folders into my backpack, slung it onto one shoulder, and excitedly began to walk toward the door to leave the school. I could hear Miguel and the boy who had been my best friend in first grade talking right behind me. I was about to turn around to talk to Miguel when I felt a small pebble hit the back of my calf. "Look how fat her calves are." And another pebble hit my calf. Inside, I wilted like a dying flower. Outside, I pretended not to hear Miguel.

He continued to throw the pebbles at my calves until I walked out the door. I fought back tears and walked quickly away to get onto my bus to go home. I proudly, silently, swallowed all my sadness and let it consume me. Even when I arrived at home, I didn't cry. I simply went to find more food to numb the pain.

HEALING WISDOM

To heal, I needed to decide that I wanted to heal. I know now that I needed to decide to be done with the pain and the torment of my soul. For so long, I allowed others to hurt me. I could have chosen any point to scream, "ENOUGH!" Each day, I have a choice to be willing to do the work of becoming self-aware, using healing tools from my counselor or life coach, and making it a practice. I am willing to show up for the work each day, but it wasn't always like this. I am willing to get up each time I fall.

QUESTIONS FOR REFLECTION

When is a time you wanted to say no, but didn't? When is a time you didn't speak up for yourself? If you had a time machine to go back to that time, what would you say?

CHAPTER SEVEN

PIANISSIMO

Pianissimo: *(π) a very quiet dynamic marking*

ABUSED

On the worst day of my childhood, the day I determined I would leave my life in Zeeland, North Dakota forever, the VanderVoot homestead held a certain tension. It was April 2000, and I was seated at the family computer desk that we had for about a year. At that time, it was an extremely rare privilege to have a family computer. The desk was in our two-part living room closest to the piano and away from the TV. We had orange shag carpet, orange curtains, and patterned wallpaper that was one of many layers of wallpaper in that room.

Back then, we used dial-up internet, which was loud and like a bad, screeching song ending in static. I remember chatting on AOL Instant Messenger with my friends, most of whom were guys. Using chat boxes to talk to friends felt so much safer than in person, and I felt free to express myself. I was happy chatting with people from all over the United States instead of just from my rural neighborhood. I used a chat room for about half an hour before my dad, who was seated in his recliner chair near the TV, began talking to me from across the room.

"Are you ever getting off that thing?" He scowled into his newspaper and barely looked at me as he said it.

"I will in a minute," I replied.

Ten seconds went by before my dad nearly growled at me. "You know, you don't have to spend all day on the computer."

I didn't say anything as I frowned and tried to finish up my conversations with friends. I could feel the tension rising from him like a dark cloud growing larger and larger above his head. When I could feel the "anger cloud" coming, I automatically began to shut down. I stopped laughing at what my friends were saying and got very quiet.

"You're being selfish!" he snapped. "All you do is stay on the computer all day! You think you're the only one who wants to use it?!" His brown eyes were flashing at this point. "Get off. Get off the computer. Get off the computer. Get off the computer. GET OFF OF THE COMPUTER!!!!!!!!!" he roared.

My sister, Sophie, timidly watched the exchange from her seat on the couch nearby.

In my extreme irritation, I abruptly stood up and threw my headphones on the ground. I was so angry at being treated this way. In the process of standing up, I accidentally knocked my chair over. I could feel my dad's rage as he looked at the chair on its side and stood up. I thought, *I will just go up to my room to get away from him. He's so annoying!*

I calmly began walking into the part of the living room where he was because, to get to my room, I needed to exit where he was, go through the kitchen, then head up the stairs to my room. I walked past him feeling irritated and already planning what I was going to write in my stories to create a different feeling. My novels were always my escape from tension and pain.

Just as I was about to leave the living room to go into the kitchen, I felt my dad's strong farmer arm grabbing me around the neck and pulling me back to him. His grip tightened as the dark cloud of rage centered over us. He squeezed and squeezed, and I could no longer breathe. Everything seemed to slow down and then stop for a while as I imagined that I was about to die. My dad strangled me. And as he did, I felt the finality of being unwanted and worthless to him. I felt that I was being thrown into the trash—just as he had thrown away the Viking football TV that I made him for Father's Day out of a cardboard box, Polaroid photo of one of the Vikings, and bent wire hanger. I truly believed that it was going to be my last day on Earth. But then suddenly he grabbed my entire body and threw me at the laundry basket near the couch where my sister sat. He screamed, "FOLD THE CLOTHES!!!" My mother exclaimed in a high-pitched voice, "Ryan! *You* fold the clothes!" There was no apology and no defending of her daughter. I felt alone in a house of six people. I knew without a doubt that I had to leave to survive.

I went to my room with tears of disbelief streaming down my face. I was in shock, and I could still feel the pressure on my neck as if my dad's arm was still squeezing the life out of me. The other point that shocked me was that my mother had not defended me at all. There was no, "Ryan! If you ever lay your hands on our daughter again, I will leave you!" Nothing other than an admonishment about the laundry. I was left to defend my own life, and my little sister, Sophie, had witnessed it all. I felt deeply disturbed.

REACHING OUT FOR HELP

The next morning, once I ensured that my dad was outside busy with calving season, I snuck down the stairs to the living room where the computer waited for me. I placed my hands gently on the chair arms, took a deep breath, and then booted up the computer. I urgently signed onto AOL Instant Messenger and found my friend Paul in my list of friends.

I sent him a message: "Paul, how are you?"

"Good, and you?"

"I'm okay. I have a question for you. I have a friend who needs some advice and I'm not sure what to tell them. They said their dad tried to strangle them and they were really upset about it. What should they do?"

For a little while, no response came. Then suddenly, "Rachel, that friend is you, isn't it?"

I swallowed hard because I felt deep shame. I felt so confused about the entire situation, especially because I felt that my family expected me to have all the answers and figure it out myself.

I responded, "Maybe."

Paul messaged back, "Let me give you a call. I'll call you in five minutes."

I was so grateful that we had a cordless phone at our house (I had grown up with a rotary phone connected to the wall). I brought the cordless phone upstairs to my room and closed the door, waiting for Paul to call.

"Hi, Paul," I said as soon as the phone rang.

He sounded upset for me. "Rachel, what happened?"

I nervously repeated what had transpired the night before. I hated describing the situation that felt like it should be a big secret never to be shared with anyone.

Paul asked me a question that pierced my heart: "You know that's child abuse, right?"

I felt so confused. I had grown up thinking that this was how all fathers treated their children. I thought all fathers judged and yelled at their children, sometimes hit them, and never said they were sorry. I quietly said into the phone, "I never thought of it that way before."

I paced across the blue carpet in my room from one wall over to my closet door. "What do I do?" I asked.

Paul lived in Massachusetts in a densely populated city. He said, "Call the police!"

I took a deep breath while looking at my closet door and sat down in my dark blue, upholstered 1980s chair with a springy cushion that made the noise of springs coiling as I sat. "I can't," I said. "We live on a farm outside of a tiny town. We have a cop that is shared in the county. I don't even know if that police officer would be around. Everyone knows everyone else's business here. If I called the police in the morning, the entire town would know about my dad by evening. I don't want to do that to my family."

Paul didn't like my answer, but he realized I wasn't changing my mind. "Well, what about your pastor? He's a man of God."

I tried to envision my pastor, a very tall man with dark hair who lived 15 miles away in South Dakota, coming to speak to me alone at my church. I was less nervous about this idea. "Maybe I could do that. I could call him and ask. I don't know his number."

"Look it up in the phone book," Paul said. At that time, we had a *White Pages* guidebook with home phone numbers for all of North Dakota and South Dakota.

We chatted for a little while longer and then ended the call. My inner compass felt broken when I wasn't talking to Paul. He felt like my lifeline, and what he said made sense. I mistakenly thought that all I could do was look for answers outside of myself.

HEALING WISDOM

Sit alone in meditation, taking deep breaths, and focus on your inner child. Go back to her in your mind's eye and hug her. Tell her comforting words and remind her that what happened was not her fault. Tell her you love her and you are always here for her.

QUESTIONS FOR REFLECTION

What would you say to the younger version of yourself right now? Would you hug them? Would you cry with them?

CHAPTER EIGHT

CYMBALS

Cymbals: *percussion instrument usually consisting of two circular brass plates struck together as a pair*

I parked my blue two-door 1986 Ford Tempo outside of the white Zeeland Reformed Church and swallowed hard as I turned off the car. I looked down at the steering wheel for a moment, then off into the horizon where cows grazed in a field on the edge of town. I got out of the car and put the keys in my pocket. Nervously, I stepped onto the sidewalk and walked past the grassy lawn and into the side door of the church. The white door stuck slightly as I pulled it open, then made a whooshing sound as I pushed it hard to close it behind me.

I found a brown metal folding chair and pulled it out to sit as I waited. The chair was cold as I waited for my pastor to arrive. I looked down at the thin, dull, brown-colored carpeting and tapped my foot impatiently. I had chosen a seat in the hallway in between the stairs leading down to the basement and the stairs leading up to the sanctuary, where I sometimes sat for Sunday School class.

Reverend Gray arrived five minutes later, his tall form ducking under the door frame as he politely nodded in my direction and moved to find a chair. He unfolded another brown metal chair and sat across from me, holding a Bible in his hand.

"Thanks for meeting me here. I didn't know who else to talk to," I said sadly.

"What's been happening?" he asked quietly. He straightened his tie and adjusted himself to sit up straighter in his seat.

My voice was already cracking as I spoke. "You might not be able to tell, but when my dad isn't at church, he's mean. He yells a lot and is always angry. Usually, he yells at me and my sisters. He hits us sometimes."

Tears started to flow down my face uncontrollably. "He calls my sister a bitch, and he kicks my other sister with his steel-toed boots. Sometimes he slaps us. He calls us stupid, worthless losers." I felt so embarrassed as I cried louder and louder. "And he tried to strangle me. I couldn't breathe. I tried to tell my mom, but she just said he is a stressed-out farmer."

Reverend Gray handed me a box of tissues. He looked at me calmly with sympathetic eyes. "Would you like me to talk to him?"

As tears streamed out of my eyes and I took breaths in between blowing my nose, I nodded my head. I asked him, "Please wait until I graduate from high school and move to Medora before you talk to him? I'll be moving there to work this summer. I don't want to be anywhere near my house when you talk to him. I'm afraid of what he will do to me."

He agreed to wait. Gently, and in a very respectful way, he gave me a hug and handed me another tissue. "I will be sure this doesn't happen again," he said.

The pastor kept his word. After I graduated high school and moved to Medora, he spoke to my dad about how my sisters and I had been treated. I wrote my dad a letter to explain that I love him, but that I had to tell someone.

My dad never wrote back or responded to the letter. To this day, he has not mentioned it. To this day, he has never said "I love you" to me.

After all of the trauma I have been through—some of which you have yet to read—I have found that the more trauma you have been through, the more love you need to discover *within yourself* to begin to shine again. You have love waiting inside of you, longing to nurture you back to health.

HEALING WISDOM

I found that acknowledging what happened and then confiding in someone I trusted was so valuable. We don't need to suffer alone. Please tell someone what you are going through, because you are not alone. Choose a friend, a family member, a teacher, a counselor, or any trustworthy person who has helped you in the past.

QUESTIONS FOR REFLECTION

Who is on your top five list of people you can confide in? If you were to tell someone what happened to you, how would you feel? What can you do to show yourself compassion after describing your difficult situations?

**I hope you never forget that no matter what others say,
you were born to shine brightly.**

CHAPTER NINE

LARGO

Largo: *a very slow, broad tempo*

I didn't know how to be in relationships, especially not with myself. I didn't realize that others weren't attracted to me because I didn't love myself.

When I was 12, I discovered a secret that I didn't reveal to my family until I was 39, for fear of repercussions. I found myself staring at girls in fashion magazines, admiring their shapes. I used to draw very shapely women with low-cut shirts, and then tear the drawings up for fear of being discovered. I buried those shredded pieces of paper deep in the trash. I felt very attracted to both boys and girls. I didn't really understand what that meant back then.

My mother had subscribed me to a Christian magazine for teens that told me that gay people are sinners. When we listened to the radio, I heard Christian news expressing concern over "gays and lesbians taking over the nation." In church, I heard about how we must pray for gay people; pray the gay away. Pray Rachel's secret away. It was blazingly clear to me that I was not allowed to like girls.

I shoved my secret down into the bottom of my soul. I told myself to focus only on liking guys romantically. I ended up with a crush on nearly every guy in my high school class and didn't dare focus on the girls around me.

I was so insecure that I had to ask seven guys to go to my senior prom until one said yes. One girl told me I looked hot at junior prom, but I wasn't interested in her as more than a friend. I was very, very lonely for a long time. When I was in high school, I used to look up at the moon at night on our farm. I used to ask myself, "Who will fall in love with me? Is he out there now? Does he exist?" I could almost hear the "Somewhere Out There" song from the 1988 movie *An American Tail*.

My first "boyfriend" was an online relationship when I was 18. I didn't kiss anyone until I was 21. I didn't have a serious boyfriend until I was 23. All I wanted was love, and love evaded me for a long time.

After my summer in Medora, I moved to Iowa for my first year of college. I remember the last day that I lived in the house on the prairie of North Dakota. I looked between the lilac bushes up at the green and white arched *Ora et Labora* sign above my bedroom windows, and I felt a rush of extreme sadness and relief. While my classmates had cried at my high school graduation, I felt a paradoxical lonely jubilation.

I was free.

During my year in Iowa, my dorm roommate told me, "Don't worry. Someday you'll have a boyfriend."

I wasn't sure if that would ever be true.

I didn't realize my love for myself was the most important kind, one that allows all other love to bloom.

First from the left: Rachel, around age 15

First from the right: Rachel in 2004

Far left: Rachel in 2006

HEALING WISDOM

Look deeply into the mirror with love. Look into your gorgeous eyes, truly into your soul. That beautiful woman has always been there—with you through everything. She has been waiting for you to witness her. She—the beautiful one who shines—is you. She has been you all along.

QUESTIONS FOR REFLECTION

How did you feel before and after the self-love exercise? How much resistance did you notice to receiving your own love? When you change your negative self-talk to self-appreciation, what changes for you?

(CHAPTER TEN)

MINOR KEY

> **Minor key:** *music based on a minor scale*
> *(traditionally considered "sad" sounding)*

#METOO

I transferred schools in my sophomore year. In my senior year at Concordia College in Moorhead, Minnesota, I lived on campus in the senior apartments with three roommates. April shared a room with me, and Sasha and Karen shared the other room. April, Sasha, and Karen had been friends before I moved in with them. At first, they were all kind to me. As time went on, April developed a bizarre jealousy of what I could only determine was a difference in our homework loads in college. I was a French major and double minor in English Writing and Religion. I sang in the choir. This meant most of the time, other than during choir practice or classes, I was doing my homework in our on-campus apartment. April was an art major and spent much of her time in the campus studio working on her art projects. Eventually, only Sasha was nice to me. At first, I was hurt by the fact that April and Karen treated me so rudely. Then, as usual, I withdrew into myself and threw a constant self-pity party. At this point, I was an expert at feeling sorry for myself and avoiding confrontation.

For a few weeks, I had been talking to a guy I met online named William. He told me the most romantic things and shared romantic songs that he said reminded him of me. At the time, I ate up all the attention. I loved how he flattered me, flirted with me, and showered me with compliments. He lived about three and a half hours away from me in Minneapolis.

"Let's meet in person," he messaged me one day. "I'll be in Fargo this weekend."

I was hesitant because I had met some strange guys in the past through online dating. However, I really liked him, and I was curious about how our chemistry would be in person. I was excited that someone, anyone, would want to date me.

We agreed to meet at the Starbucks café inside the Barnes & Noble in Moorhead.

FIRST DATE

On the day that we agreed to meet, I picked out my favorite long-sleeved, sheer, brown Express shirt with small pink flowers on it. The shirt tied shut at the top with criss-crossed suede laces. I wore a brown camisole underneath and a pair of nice jeans. My hair had finally grown past my chin, and I held it back with a soft brown headband. Excitedly, I parked in the Barnes & Noble parking lot and headed inside to find William.

He was nowhere to be found, so I went ahead and ordered a Grande Mocha Latte. I waited for my drink while looking through a turnstile of books.

"Hey there." He interrupted my thoughts with a tap on my shoulder. William was from Zimbabwe, slightly taller than my 5'5" frame, and well-dressed. He wore sunglasses. "Are you Rachel?"

"I am. You're William?"

"Yeah, I got us a table over here."

We sat down across from each other, and William put his food and drink on the table. He had a dessert that required a spoon.

"How was your drive?" I asked.

"It was fine. Want a bite?" William held out a spoon full of his dessert that was topped with a melted marshmallow substance.

I felt so confused as he asked me the question. I was meeting William for the first time, and here he was offering me a spoon of his food that his mouth had already been on. The Rachel I was at that time was really unfamiliar with boundaries (what were those?), and so I accepted.

He smiled crookedly and said, "My ex-girlfriend loved sharing desserts with me. I'll show you a picture of her. She's a model." William showed me a photo of a woman posing on rocks near a stream. "You know, even though we broke up, she still likes to sleep with me. But I stopped seeing her. I'm just here for you, baby."

While I should have figuratively wiped the slime off my ears, I was taken by how well he was dressed and the smell of his cologne. I didn't value myself very much at the time. I was just excited that a man was paying attention to me.

DRUNK

"You know what, let's get out of here," William said.

I looked at him with a surprised expression. "But we just got here!"

"I know, but I really don't want to hang out at a café. Let's go somewhere fun." He adjusted his position in an overconfident, cocky way as if he knew I was going to say yes to anything he asked.

"Where do you want to go? I'm okay with going to a private place," I said, ignoring the tense feeling in my belly.

"Let's go to a bar! We'll have a good time there." William smiled widely.

"Fine, I'll meet you there." I was skeptical but I thought, *What can one or two drinks hurt?* It was my chance to get to know him better.

I have a very clear memory of, after having a couple of drinks at the bar with him, seeing a sign in the bathroom warning about the date rape drug. I remember having a sinking feeling as I read the sign on the wall. I thought, *Should I be concerned?*

When I returned to the table, William had already ordered me another rum and coke. He kept ordering me more drinks until I had about four. I was very drunk at this point and unable to drive.

"I'll drive," William happily volunteered.

"Take me to my apartment, please."

"I don't want to go to your apartment. I want to go to my hotel," he said.

"I really don't want to go to your hotel. Please take me back to my apartment."

William smiled more widely. "I tell you what. I can see it's better if I drive, and we can talk about it in the car!"

I slurred something as I grabbed my purse and wobbled after him heading outdoors.

When I was seated in the car and William was on the road, he looked over at me intensely and said, "You have really nice lips."

"Thaaanks," I slurred, leaning against the car door.

"You have such nice lips that I want to see your other pair of lips." William licked his lips.

I was so naïve and quite drunk that I didn't understand at first. "Are we going to my apartment? My roommates are there. It will be nice for you to meet them."

"We're going to my hotel."

"I told you, uh, I really don't want to go…to your hotel," I slurred. I felt completely confused and unable to make wise decisions.

"Relax! We can sit down and talk. It will be really nice. I'll give you a back rub."

I hesitated. My brain felt like sludge as I tried to think about what to say. "Okayyyy. As long as we're just talking. Talking's gooood."

HOTEL

Although my memory is foggy, I do remember that when we arrived at the hotel check-in desk, William gave them a last name that was different from what he had told me. The woman repeated the name back to him, and my brain slowly registered that the names were different.

In the hotel room, he took a quick phone call while I sat on the bed and watched some TV. I was secretly panicking a little inside because I didn't know what to expect. I was just so inexperienced and naïve.

"Let me give you a backrub, baby," he said when his phone call was over.

"Okayyy." I closed my eyes as he rubbed my back.

Suddenly, he was taking my clothes off. I told him, "I want to keep my clothes on."

"Relax, baby. You're going to like this."

I was so tired and drunk that I laid back on the bed. He kept removing my clothes as I was lying there half awake. William got on top of me and took off his clothes too. I felt a sharp pain between my legs and confusion as I opened my eyes.

"I want to get dressed," I said.

"You're so fine, baby, you know you like it. I'm going to go use the bathroom and when I get back, you'll be ready for me, won't you?" William smiled wider and wider, then winked at me.

As I became more sober, I felt disgusting. When he went into the bathroom, I slowly put my clothes back on. With some confusion, I noticed the blood in my underwear. I wasn't quite registering what was happening to me. Just as I was fully dressed, William came back into the room.

"Oh, let's take care of that, we need to take care of that." William started to take my clothes off again.

"I don't waaant to get undressed."

"Rachel, I want to see those sweet lips again, relax baby."

I felt upset, but I closed my mouth and I let him undress me again. I didn't want any part of this, but I was in such shock that I didn't know how to say no. I didn't know how to get away. I was too drunk to drive and felt too far along in the moment to turn back. I felt powerless. Instead of defending myself, I let him have his way. Inside I was screaming, but on the outside I was quiet. I was slipping away, out of my body, out of this room, focusing on something or anything else until it was over. I wanted to write my way out of this story.

When he was done with me, William lay back on the bed with a smile on his face. I quietly got dressed and placed my headband back onto my hair.

I tied the front of my shirt after pulling it over my camisole. I felt awkward, and I didn't want to stay a moment longer.

BLAMING THE VICTIM

"Can you take me home now?"

William agreed to take me back to my campus apartment. As we drove back over the bridge and into Moorhead to my college campus, I stared out of the window of my car with immense sadness. I felt so disappointed in myself and ashamed. William dropped me off, got into his own car, and said he would call me later.

I reached into my pocket to take out the keys to my apartment. At that moment, I realized I didn't have them. A couple of days prior, I had gotten into a car accident with some twins while pulling out of my snowbank-filled parking lot. My apartment keys were attached to my car keys, which were at the auto mechanic. The car keys I had were from a vehicle I was borrowing from my parents. I had no way of getting into my apartment.

I called the apartment from my cell phone. No one answered. I couldn't believe this was happening to me.

Feeling half drunk and completely frozen, I crossed the street to the main part of campus and made my way to my sister Sophie's dorm. She gave me a hug as I came into the room, and tears spilled down my face.

"Sophie, I think I was raped."

We talked about what happened until late into the night, and I fell asleep on her roommate's empty bunk bed. Thankfully, her roommate was out for the night.

In the morning, I hugged my sister close and then walked back to my apartment. This time when I called the apartment phone, April answered. "Oh, you're back," she said flatly.

When April let me in, I sat down on the living room couch and started crying. "I can't believe he did that," I said.

"I tried to tell you not to go with him to the hotel," April said with an annoyed tone in her voice. "You know this is your fault, right?"

Her words hurt like a knife in my heart. I couldn't believe that April was blaming me. Yes, I had willingly gone to the hotel—after William bought me multiple drinks with the intention of getting me drunk enough to sleep with me. I sat in stunned silence and pain. Maybe April was right. I felt so confused. Maybe I was the one to blame. Maybe this was all my fault. I tried to hide my tears from April as she rolled her eyes and went into our bedroom.

I sat quietly on the couch, sopping up my tears with tissues. I felt very, very alone. April didn't seem to care at all, and when the other roommates found out, they stopped talking to me completely.

I spent decades blaming myself, despite therapy. A therapist in college told me that William clearly planned the entire thing. I finally understood that he was to blame, not me, when I wrote this chapter.

HEALING WISDOM

Write about what happened. Write a letter to that person or those people, but don't actually give it to them. Their actions were not sacred, and yet they have light within them. Yes, even "monsters" have some light in them, it's just so hard to see it through their immensely dark and terrible actions. When you have finished the letter, safely burn it in a sink or cauldron. Scatter or bury the ashes outside.

QUESTIONS FOR REFLECTION

What would you say to the person who caused you trauma if you could say everything in your heart and mind? How do you think you will feel when the letter is written and burned?

CHAPTER ELEVEN

ACCELERANDO

Accelerando: *gradually speeding up the speed of the rhythmic beat*

In 2005, I received a call that changed my life. I was finishing my day at work in the corporate world at Unisys in Bismarck when my mother called me.

"Your uncle is in jail."

My Uncle Frankie, born in the island nation of Papua New Guinea, had lived in Washington State for 30 years. Most years, he and my Aunt Patty drove with my three cousins all the way from Washington to North Dakota for Christmas. My aunts, uncles, cousins, and my family gathered each year at my grandparents' house at Christmas. We were raised to know that family was very valued.

I was shocked. "What happened?" I asked as I gathered up my purse and coat and headed out the door to the parking lot where my car was. All I could think of was that my uncle was schizophrenic and vulnerable as a result.

"Apparently, someone stole Uncle Frankie's wallet. When your aunt went to report it at the police station, because the wallet had your uncle's green card in it, the police took your uncle into custody. He will spend three months in jail due to the Patriot Act," my mom said solemnly. The Patriot Act had been enacted after the September 11th terrorist attack on New York City.

"But he's not a terrorist!" I exclaimed.

"I know." My mom was quiet.

I decided at that moment that I could either spend the rest of my life being angry about what was happening, or I could do something about it. I could turn my anger into action.

I knew I couldn't directly help my uncle, but I did some research and found the perfect graduate school to help me make an impact. The School for International Training (now the SIT Graduate Institute) offered a master's program combining Social Justice in Intercultural Relations PLUS a year in the Peace Corps. I decided that the best way to bring social justice to situations like my uncle's was to obtain my master's degree and make a positive difference through my career.

In the fall of 2006, I packed my car to the brim and drove with a friend across half of the United States—from North Dakota to Brattleboro, Vermont—to learn how to make the world a better place.

I learned how to help many people before also learning how to help myself.

HEALING WISDOM

Root yourself in your circumstances as they are (masculine) and then choose magical thinking (feminine) to rise into your higher self. Your physical and spiritual bodies are connected as one on this earth. With this imagery, we are as trees needing to grow into the ground and up into the light.

QUESTIONS FOR REFLECTION

How do you know when you need a break? What can you do to fuel your own soul? While helping others is wonderful and sometimes necessary, how often do you ask for help? How often have you said no when you really needed to?

CHAPTER TWELVE

SYNCOPATION

Syncopation: *an "off-the-beat" accent*

The tears fall quickly as I write these words. I almost didn't write these next few chapters because of the immense pain from remembering. But I need to reveal it for my healing, and perhaps for yours.

Since high school, I have wanted to join the Peace Corps. I remember a tall man with glasses from the Peace Corps coming to talk to my high school English class. He spoke of faraway places and told sparkling stories of cultures and languages so far outside the scope of my small mid-western town. He spoke of travel in places without flat land, of aromatic foods, of living with people who wove a rich tapestry of diverse wisdom and character. His descriptions drew me to his words like a magnet until I could feel the most ultimate excitement bubbling up, waiting to spill across my lips in joy. When this man asked, "Who wants more information about joining the Peace Corps?" I wanted to jump up and yell out, "ME! OH YES, ME!!!" Instead, I looked around in surprise that no one raised their hand. I self-consciously and hesitantly raised my hand, which was very brave for me at the time. I felt the glow and the promise of being paid to travel to foreign lands.

After I finished my bachelor's degree and worked for a couple of years, I dressed up in my favorite faux fur vest and drove by myself from Bismarck all the way to downtown Minneapolis to interview for the Peace Corps. For someone who grew up on a farm and learned how to drive on a gravel road, the fact that I drove by myself and parked in the downtown of a city of 420,000 people with no help made me feel a sense of pride. I did it all for the Peace Corps.

In graduate school, when I traveled to D.C. to volunteer for the American-Arab Anti-Discrimination Committee (ADC), I met with a director of the Peace Corps for lunch. I continually requested Peace Corps Morocco until I got it. I was in! My dream was going to come true. I imagined all the people I would help.

With only a month left to go before flying to Morocco, I had no idea how much my life was about to change.

HEALING WISDOM

Although I had big dreams that I had every right to pursue, I wasn't prepared for a change in the trajectory of my path. When thrown off course, I learned that healing is a journey, not a destination. At times, you will feel so completely healed, and then something will happen to reopen a part of your wound.

QUESTION FOR REFLECTION

How would you feel if you learned to process life as it is instead of how you expect it to be?

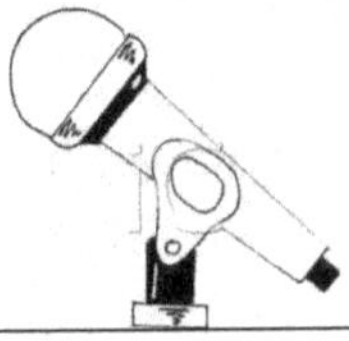

CHAPTER THIRTEEN

SFORZANDO

Sforzando (ß): *sudden stress on a note or chord*

PEACE CORPS DREAMS

Flat Street Pub was busy that Friday night. The sounds of laughter and glasses clinking together rose above the hum of conversation as my friends Monica and Alicia walked with me through the doors of the pub in Brattleboro, Vermont. At the end of a long week, I was excited to meet new people and relax. Immediately, I saw someone from my Policy Advocacy class who waved me over to talk.

"Hey Rachel!" he beamed.

"Jordan! How are you?"

We chatted excitedly about the on-campus phase of graduate school ending, our plans for our internships, and the local microbrew options on the menu. My friends Monica and Alicia were busy connecting with other friends from our dorm who happened to be there.

Jordan was set to intern in Thailand, and I had already been accepted by the Peace Corps in Morocco. I had spent a year studying Arabic and a few

phrases of Tachelhit. This was the year I was going to make my dream come true! I told Jordan about how just a month prior, I had shared lunch with a Peace Corps Director in Washington, D.C. And back when I lived in North Dakota, I had driven by myself all the way from tiny town ND to downtown Minneapolis for my interview. I was driven and determined to make it to Morocco, just as I had applied myself enough to study and live in France.

Jordan interrupted my Peace Corps thoughts by calling one of his friends over. "Yusef, I haven't seen you in such a long time. Where have you been?"

Yusef joined us and introduced himself. He was just slightly taller than me, with short black hair and a dark complexion. "I've been in Nigeria visiting my family, Jordan." I noticed his eyes were a deep brown and instantly felt drawn to him. Jordan, Yusef, and I talked for a little while before Yusef had to leave. I felt a slight disappointment that he didn't ask for my phone number because I was feeling quite flirtatious.

Later that week, I was having dinner at a Greek sandwich shop with my friend Monica. We were seated at a booth in the tiny sandwich depot when suddenly I noticed that Yusef was standing right by our table. He locked eyes with me and asked, "What are you doing tonight? You need to make plans to be with me."

I smiled and said, "Apparently, I am going on a date with you. Can you meet me at 8:00 pm?"

"I will see you then at Flat Street Pub," he said.

"See you there."

Monica smiled at me and winked, "Ohhh!"

I laughed a little, feeling giddy because I felt excited about the idea of going on a date. Just a few months prior, I had almost become engaged to an Egyptian man and then broke off the engagement. We had a long-distance relationship, so to be able to date someone in person made me very happy.

ENGAGED

That night, while wearing my peach dress, I met Yusuf at Flat Street Pub. I liked him immediately. He was a handsome Nigerian with black hair, dark eyes, and a preference for wearing soccer jerseys. He was a little intense, but very intriguing. We had a couple of drinks, then went off to his apartment.

From the very first date, Yusuf was asking me to marry him. I thought it was strange because I barely knew him. I said no, and with each additional date he persisted. I told him, "I can't marry you! I'm going to Morocco for the Peace Corps."

Yusuf begged me, "Please, I love you. I know you love me. We can spend the rest of our lives together."

Each time I turned Yusuf down, he pleaded more. With each date, he asked again. I began wondering what to do because I was developing strong feelings for him.

In my mind, I rationalized that what I would do is get engaged, go to Morocco, and then if it didn't work out, we could break off the engagement. Or, if it did work out, we would get married.

On perhaps our tenth date, I met Yusuf and his friend, Rex, at Flat Street Pub. Rex had brought his very obnoxious friend with him who spoke loudly at the bar about Viagra and sex. Rex's friend was nearly kicked out by the bartender.

Suddenly, Yusuf told me he needed to show me something in the basement of the Flat Street Pub. He brought me downstairs, got down on one knee, and pulled out a box with an amethyst and diamond ring. "Rachel, will you marry me?"

I said yes. One week later, I found out I was pregnant.

HEALING WISDOM

Call upon your angels and guides. Ask the Universe for guidance and you will hear whispers of wisdom—if you trust. I have received many random pieces of wisdom whispered to my heart from my angels and guides. Light a candle and watch how it dances or burns steadily upright.

QUESTIONS FOR REFLECTION

When unexpected things happen to you, where can you go for peace? If you can't go anywhere, what kind of meditation or prayer, if any, do you like to practice? Have you tried counseling? Has it been helpful?

CHAPTER FOURTEEN

LULLABY

Lullaby: *a quiet, gentle song sung to send a child to sleep*

My son is my greatest joy. Yet he almost didn't exist.

A week after getting engaged, I drove nervously and scared by myself to the Planned Parenthood in Brattleboro. My health insurance from grad school had lapsed now that it was summer, I was unemployed, and I still needed to buy my plane ticket to Rabat, Morocco for the Peace Corps. As a result, Planned Parenthood was my only affordable option because they accepted donations. I gave them all I had, which was $11.

The night before, I had taken two positive pregnancy tests that I just didn't want to believe. My heart was focused on my dream of traveling to Morocco. My assignment was to work with rural textile workers with micro-credit to help them increase their income. Pregnancy was a situation I just hadn't planned for.

When the nurse at Planned Parenthood confirmed that I was indeed pregnant, my breath stuck in my throat and I forced myself to become numb. I could barely focus as she talked about my options of giving birth, giving the baby up for adoption, or having an abortion. I felt sick if I focused too much on what she was saying because I didn't know what to do. I told her I would think about what was next, and she gave me pamphlets of information about all my options.

After I left the building, sat in my blue Buick, and set my pamphlets and green Guess purse down on the seat next to me, I sat still. I sat very, very still in the silence of my car. I peered over the steering wheel to the bushes that surrounded the parking lot. I turned on the car to hear The Chicks CD begin playing the song "Lullaby."

My tears were like a waterfall drowning me. With each tear that streamed down my face, I felt a desperation in my soul. I couldn't have this baby. I needed to fulfill my dream. But I felt torn because I had always told myself I would be responsible and keep the baby if I unexpectedly got pregnant.

And the song played on. I drove out of the parking lot and down the street, barely being able to see and crying as I heard the song. I tried to sing, but my voice kept breaking.

HEALING WISDOM

Using your heart as a portal, sit in meditation and travel back to yourself as a child. Greet her with love and ask her what bothers her. Listen to what she has to say and be sure to write it down in your journal after your meditation is complete. Hold her and comfort her. Assure your child-self that she is safe and protected, and she is loved. If you have been attuned to Reiki, give her a Reiki session. Slowly, the feeling of peace will fill you and the anxiety of the past will begin to drift away. You can create a new beginning for yourself that is not defined by what happened in the past.

QUESTIONS FOR REFLECTION

How do you feel after you come out of meditation? If your younger self could talk to you, what would she say? What is a lesson you can learn from difficult choices?

CHAPTER FIFTEEN

A CAPPELLA

A Cappella: *(adj.) sung without instrumental accompaniment*

I swallowed my dreams of joining the Peace Corps as I drove from little Brattleboro, Vermont to Manchester, the largest city in New Hampshire. The large three-lane highways going north and south lined with pine trees and the cars speeding by only heightened my anxiety as I drove by myself. It was just me and my pregnant belly as Yusef had to finish working for a couple more weeks in Brattleboro before joining me.

I reached back to grab something from the crowded back seat. My car was packed with absolutely everything that would fit into it, including all my belongings that I had used in grad school. I had my Guess purse on the seat next to me, which I rummaged through until I found my cell phone. I decided to call my new landlord. Yusef and I had just signed a lease to rent a single room in a shared house—with no storage space. It was all that was in our budget at the time.

The landlord didn't answer. Each time I called, the phone went to voicemail. I called for the next hour with no success.

"I'll call my sister Sophie's boyfriend, Rex," I said. Rex answered the phone, and I explained that the new landlord wasn't taking my phone calls and I needed a new place to stay.

"Sure, yeah, you can stay here. Just give me a call this afternoon when I'm off work and I'll meet you at my place."

"Great, thanks Rex!" I said in relief.

I drove through Manchester until I found a Barnes & Noble to pass the time. I ordered a mocha latte and a sandwich, read through magazines and books, and wandered around looking at calendars and journals. Finally, after a couple of hours had passed, I decided to go out to my car and call Rex at the scheduled time.

He didn't answer. At all. For the rest of the night.

For hours, I sat cramped with my pregnant belly behind the steering wheel of my car. I started to panic because I realized that at that moment, I had become homeless. I had nowhere to stay. I didn't have a credit card and my bank account was empty. I began to cry tears of shame. Finally, after crying for what felt like half an hour, I called my mom. To my immense relief, my mother paid for me to stay at a hotel.

The next morning, I started my new internship resettling refugees.

HEALING WISDOM

Let go with the elements as an act of love for yourself. After you have stopped weeping, go into a quiet room and be gentle with yourself. Hold your hands over your heart and use the Hawaiian tradition of forgiveness. Say the words of the Hawaiian ho'oponopono blessing to yourself: "I love you. I'm sorry. Please forgive me. Thank you." Give yourself the compassion that you expected so many times from others but never received. You are worthy of all the love that exists. You are love, and you deserve love.

QUESTIONS FOR REFLECTION

Where in your schedule can you carve out time to spend in nature? When in your day can you set aside time for a luxurious bath? How else can you nurture yourself when you are filled with sorrow?

CHAPTER SIXTEEN

TRILL

Trill: *rapid alternation of two close pitches to create a "shaking" ornament on a melodic note*

LIVING IN POVERTY

The first night in my Manchester apartment, I slept on the floor because I didn't have a bed. I could hear gunshots in the distance that I hoped were fireworks. I slept restlessly by myself on the floor of my second-floor apartment.

After a couple of weeks by myself in the apartment, Yusuf moved in. I was a Christian, and he was a Muslim. At first, we were happy newlyweds. My parents bought me a bed because Yusuf was not yet employed and I was making an intern's stipend. We were young, in love, and thought that love would solve everything.

I began questioning our marriage when I noticed how much Yusuf was drinking. On average, I was cleaning up six empty Guinness bottles per day from our apartment. At first, Yusuf was fully functional despite all this drinking. He got and kept a job.

ALCOHOLISM

In 2008, my beautiful baby boy was born with a full head of dark, curly hair. When I saw his face, I discovered an entirely new kind of love. I made payments on a Bose speaker just so I could play my iPod playlist during Gabriel's birth. Holding Gabriel brought tears to my eyes, and I felt like the luckiest mom in the world.

After our son Gabriel was born, I noticed that Yusuf had added brandy to his drinking routine. Sometimes his friend Rex, who was dating my sister Sophie, came over to drink brandy with Yusuf. A few times, Yusuf got fired from jobs. We ended up being on Food Stamps/SNAP benefits.

When we moved from Manchester to Pembroke for my new job as an employment counselor, Yusuf was drinking so heavily that he usually passed out by 6:00 pm every night. One morning at around 3:00 am, a loud knock at the door startled me awake. Yusuf had been in Vermont at a wedding, and I thought it was a strange hour for anyone to knock.

I stumbled out of bed and went to the front door. I squinted and could see through the glass that it was a police officer. I attempted to open the door, but struggled because I had a childproof cover on the doorknob to prevent my baby from going outside. Finally, after struggling and fumbling, I opened the door.

"Hello," I said with confusion to the officer.

"Hello, are you Yusuf's wife?" the police officer asked with a very cold stare. He was bald, thin, and not much taller than me.

"Yes."

"We're going to need you to come down to the police station," the officer said.

"What happened?" I asked.

"Your husband is in jail," he said coldly. "He was pulled over for drunk driving. You can bail him out for $75, but you will need to bring cash. You'll need to come down to the police station in Concord where we have him. His license has been suspended."

I was in shock. I managed to choke out, "Thank you," before he left.

In the darkness, I gathered my baby up into my arms from his crib and placed him in the car seat to bring him with me to pick up his dad. At first, I was so angry at Yusuf. Then he told me a story about how the police officer had arrested him because she was racist. However, the police report revealed he had been driving under the influence.

For the next year, I drove Yusuf where he needed to go because he didn't have a license.

When Yusuf had a job again, he spent all his hours working or being passed-out drunk.

I will never forget the day that Yusuf brought Gabriel with him to Rex and my sister Sophie's house, which happened to be just up the street. Gabriel was about three years old. Rex and Yusuf had been drinking together, as usual, and they were very drunk. I was visiting with Sophie at my place, and we decided to go outside. As I looked up the street, I couldn't believe what I was seeing. Yusuf and I lived at the bottom of a hill, and as I looked up the street, I could see Gabriel running down it by himself. He was in the middle of the street. I panicked and started to run toward him.

"Gabriel!" I cried out.

There behind him, seemingly without a care in the world, were Yusuf and Rex, laughing and paying no attention to Gabriel.

I was so angry. I ran up the hill and scooped Gabriel into my arms. "Yusuf!" I frowned. "Yusuf, you're supposed to be watching our son!"

He poked Rex's side and they both started whispering and laughing. "Relax!" Yusuf said. "Errrrrything's fiiine. We're jus' havin' a good time," he slurred. I was shocked that he didn't seem to care at all.

I took Gabriel into the house. A couple of hours later, Yusuf passed out on his chair in the living room. I didn't know my husband anymore. Or maybe I hadn't really known him to begin with. I cried that night and began to grieve the marriage I saw falling apart in front of my eyes.

HEALING WISDOM

The only way to heal the pain is to go through it. Grieve. Go through the waves of grief, crash right into them as they crash into you. Get angry about what happened! I remember somewhat holding my anger back with Yusuf because I didn't want to be "too mean." But it's OKAY to get angry when your boundaries are violated! Go for a drive with music turned up, and scream and cry with as many curse words as you want. Let the tears cleanse you. What happened to you is not your fault.

QUESTIONS FOR REFLECTION

Do you allow yourself time to grieve? Where do you feel your grief or anger in your body? How do you feel after you tried some of the above ways of grieving?

(CHAPTER SEVENTEEN)

TUTTI

Tutti: *(Italian for "all" or "everyone") an indication for all performers to play together*

Regardless of what was happening at home, I was determined to get a good job. I knew I couldn't count on my husband staying employed since he had been fired from multiple jobs. I prayed for wisdom, asking for help beyond my understanding.

An inner voice told me, "Dress the part for the interview. Dress as if you have the job offer already."

I didn't have any professional clothes, and I didn't have much money. But I had some, and so I bought a new pair of pants, my first blazer, and a dress shirt at JCPenney. At the time, Yusuf and I were sharing an SUV. He was employed as a caregiver in the community for a man with disabilities, and part of his responsibility was to drive the participant around in our car. On the day of the interview, I rode in the back seat as the participant was in the front seat. I chose to believe that good things were possible.

After I got the job, I started working at the welfare office. My coworkers were kind, patient, and had the best New England sense of humor. My ears were wide open to the New England way after living in North Dakota for so long. The sarcastic jokes, adding "R" to the end of words that end in vowels, calling a purse a "pocketbook," and the phrase "wicked pissah" were just a few of the treasures I discovered.

At first, I was shy and quiet around them. Then as time went on, because Conan, Jada, Delphine, and Vicky were so easy to work with, I felt safe to be myself. As I practiced being myself, I gained confidence. And as I gained confidence, I started to become my true self.

This confidence led me to question things in my life I had never questioned before, such as my thoughts. I was taking a shower at home one day, and suddenly an internal voice said to me, "What if I could find a way to arrange my thoughts? They're always so jumbled, always full of anxiety and songs. What if I could change that?"

I became curious about this idea, so I Googled "control thoughts" on my laptop. (I didn't yet have a smart phone in 2011.) Meditation and mindfulness appeared as results. My memories flashed back to the Christian magazine my mother had subscribed me to as a teenager that described these things as "new age" and evil. I felt nervous to pursue the understanding of these things, so simply out of fear, I didn't try them until years later.

HEALING WISDOM

Confidence is a practice. I learned that the more I practiced being confident in myself, the more that others became confident in me. I wasn't always as confident as I am now. For example, I used to listen to a radio show host on NPR and think that I could never measure up to her. Then, years later, I ended up in the same regular cycling class at the same gym as her. I went from thinking I wasn't as good as her, to realizing we are both wonderful in our own individual ways.

QUESTIONS FOR REFLECTION

If you could be admired for great work in something, what would it be? What happens when you envision yourself already having accomplished this great work? How does it feel?

CHAPTER EIGHTEEN

DIRGE

Dirge: *a lament for the dead, especially one forming part of a funeral rite*

TRISHA

The turning point to my religious beliefs happened when my friend Trisha passed away. She was only 34 years old when her seven-year-old daughter found her lifeless body. After Trisha died, I couldn't bring myself to go to the same church we had gone to. I tried a couple of other churches, but it wasn't the same. My son and her daughter had gone to daycare together as toddlers. I grieved the loss of my friend.

Shortly after she died, I experienced what some would say was Trisha's spirit. She did a couple of things to get my attention. This became the beginning of my spiritual awakening. I would never see things in the same way again.

The first event happened when I visited a local crystal shop. For some time, I had felt called to go to that store. As I entered the store, I noticed that a woman working there looked familiar. And then I remembered I had met her at Trisha's funeral. She had worked with Trisha and was the owner of the crystal shop.

I learned many new things about spiritual healing, crystals, tarot cards, and all the things that my mother had forbidden. I was intrigued and felt drawn to learn everything I could. I remember that when I first called upon the angels and had a tarot reading, I truly believed something awful would happen. Would God's hand come down and shake his finger at me? Nothing bad happened. Instead, I felt free.

About a week after meeting Trisha's former colleague, my son accidentally broke my laptop. I looked online to see if I could find any local laptops for sale from a private seller. Sure enough, the person I ended up buying a laptop from lived right next to where Trisha had lived, and his family was good friends with hers.

Out of all the people who would have a laptop for sale, what were the odds they would be Trisha's neighbor?

Later, I consulted at least three mediums to ask them about Trisha. Each time, they shared that Trisha was still with me at times and that she was supporting me from "the other side."

LISTENING TO MY SOUL

After Trisha passed away in 2015, I learned about meditation techniques. A year later, I went with my son to a mindfulness camp in western New Hampshire. There, I practiced meditation and mindfulness and learned about the Buddhist monk Thich Nhat Hanh. I learned how to slow down and truly hear my soul, my inner voice. I realized that much of my anxiety came from ignoring my inner voice. Ignoring my inner voice meant I was not fully loving myself.

I didn't learn to love myself in a linear fashion; it was a long journey. I spent many years believing the lies that others told me: "You're not good enough. You're too big for that. You're not smart enough. You should just be grateful that anyone likes you."

Looking back, I would have told myself so much earlier, "You are enough. Your heart is too big to be treated that way. You are smarter than you know. You are someone who anyone would be lucky to know." Instead, I decided one day that I was done being miserable. I decided this on several different occasions. And each time, I chose the law of attraction (decide, believe, receive) to spark the start or rise of my healing journey of love. I learned about the law of attraction from Esther and Jerry Hicks' book *Ask and It Is Given*. Their philosophy suggests that positive thoughts attract positive events, and negative thoughts attract negative events. Through changing our thought process, we can influence our outcomes.

The most important step is to choose yourself. You must choose yourself over and over again. You must learn to fight for yourself. You must learn that YOU are worth fighting for. You are an amazing creation with a unique set of gifts for the world.

HEALING MYSELF

Part of my self-love was rooted in counseling. A counselor told me about thought-stopping and becoming aware of our thoughts. She taught me how to flip negative thoughts into positive ones. I realized that my dad's negative words to me growing up had continued to follow me and manifested as my inner voice. And as I became aware and began to change that inner voice, my outer actions began to change.

I signed up for many kinds of training. I read books on leadership. I remained *open* to learning as a journey and not a destination. I studied how people I admire lived their lives. I began taking care of my nutrition and my fitness. I went running during lunch time. I stopped eating fast food and drinking soda. I began to buy organic food.

The year my gallbladder was removed, just two years before my separation from my first husband, I had to learn how to eat differently because I could no longer eat the way I used to without getting sick. I went to a naturopath doctor for the first time. When I told her that I was miserable in my job at that time, she told me, "It's because you're a healer."

With each new experience, I gained a little more confidence. Slowly, bit by bit, I began to view myself differently. When I decided I would lose 60 pounds, I looked in the mirror and began to excitedly visualize becoming my future, healthier self. The trick was how I *thought* about myself. I worked on reversing my limiting beliefs. And I lost that weight.

I began to harness the power of my thoughts through meditation. At first, I could only meditate for a couple of minutes. Then four minutes. Eventually, I increased my time and tried different kinds of meditation. With patience and practice, I began to expand my consciousness and realize that all self-imposed limitations are a lie. Limitations set by others on *me* are a lie. When I cleared my false beliefs, I created space for new, supportive beliefs to enter. I began to believe I am unstoppable.

HELPING OTHERS HEAL

In 2017, I became certified in reading angel cards and a Reiki Master; in 2018, a certified holistic life coach; and in 2020, I became certified in Transcendental Meditation. In 2021, I began to further trust my inner voice, and my spiritual knowing accelerated. I discovered my mediumship abilities (communicating with loved ones who have passed on) and remembered that I am a witch. I didn't so much experience a particular memory; it was more of an inner awakening to that aspect of myself. I felt a deep knowing. I contacted my friend Bianca who is a witch, and we discovered through conversation over coffee that I instinctively know how to perform rituals and do and know so many things that most "baby" witches do not. I wouldn't be surprised if, secretly, it runs in my blood.

Sometimes, the most difficult part of the process of loving myself was receiving. If I faltered at all on my beliefs, I didn't receive what I desired. And then I had to start over. This is how meditation, patience, and practice became so valuable to me. Finally, when I added positive affirmations to my practice, I began to accelerate the manifestation of my goals. Decide. Believe. Receive. And NEVER GIVE UP.

I would be doing myself and my readers a disservice if I didn't mention the importance of forgiveness during the process of learning to love yourself. First, I had to forgive myself for treating myself so terribly because of my traumatic experiences. Next, I had to work on forgiving my dad and others who wronged me. This did NOT mean I *accepted* their behaviors. It meant that I *let go* of my clinging to the rage within me. The rage only poisoned me; it did nothing to make anyone pay for their actions.

With each forgiveness, I allowed space for more love to enter my heart. I allowed space for others to love me. I allowed room for me to love myself.

Loving yourself is a practice and a journey. When you open yourself to love, miracles begin to happen. This is how I blossomed from a wallflower into a rose.

HEALING WISDOM

I am sharing some of my inner knowledge and some knowledge gained through reading or experience here. The Earth herself holds the secrets of healing within all her elements. Walk barefoot on her, close your eyes, and find the root of your pain. Weep into your bath water. Let me say that again: sob big cries into your bath. Let it out. You must let it go or your pain will consume you. Breathe the beautiful air as deeply in and out as you can during meditation or yoga. Let the rage, pain, sadness, and confused hurt go into the earth. Let it drain out of you with the bathtub water. Scream and cry into the wind or as you are driving your car. Let it burn away. Give it to the earth, give it to the heavens, let the Universe take it from you. Stand in a forest and lean against a tree. Close your eyes and feel how nature holds and supports you in love.

QUESTIONS FOR REFLECTION

What are the unique gifts you bring to the world? If you began to choose healing, how much more energy would you have to share these gifts with others?

CHAPTER NINETEEN

DUET

Duet: *a performance by two people, especially singers, instrumentalists, or dancers*

When I finally learned to love myself, I began to view the world differently. On a frigid day in January 2012, and in the fifth year of my marriage to Yusef, I looked at my coworker, Conan, with new eyes. We had worked together for two years as friends, but something happened. It was like a bolt of lightning that hit me one day as I saw him, and I thought, "Damn. He is fine."

I tried to push the thoughts away. I shoved them down, ignored them, but these brand new feelings kept bubbling to the surface in delicious waves of curiosity of what it would be like to be with such a funny, caring, handsome man. I knew these feelings were wrong because I was married, yet I couldn't control that I indeed was falling for him.

I had watched for years as Conan was kind to everyone he met. He was witty, handsome, and a gentleman. Like me, Conan was passionate about helping refugees. We both talked about how wonderful it would be to start a nonprofit to provide resources for refugees. He was clearly a family man and had photos of his two children at his desk.

I imagined what it would be like to flirt with him. The safest way, I decided, was to enlist the help of a client who volunteered for my team in the welfare office where Conan and I worked. Part of her job was to deliver the mail to each member of our team, and so I pulled Lindsey aside and concocted a brilliant plan with her. I created an anonymous letter from a secret admirer, kissed it with my red lipstick, and gave it to Lindsey to deliver to Conan with the regular mail.

Other methods of flirtation involved hiding his case of Mountain Dew cans or tossing paper clips over the cubicle wall to get his attention. One of Conan's least favorite methods of my flirting was when I threw blueberries over the wall and he rolled back over them. For some reason, he wasn't a fan of the blueberries smashed into the floor beneath his chair!

Conan played it cool with me for what felt like an eternity, and honestly, he did not return my flirtation for most of that year. In July, he revealed to my team that he had separated from his wife in June. He was living with his grandmother. The day I found out in July, I told Conan in his cubicle, "I'm so sorry. If you need anything at all, please let me know."

In August, he let me know that he wanted to meet me for a date. I met Conan in the parking lot of Shorty's Mexican Restaurant in Hooksett, only to find that it was closed. I got into Conan's car trembling, wearing a short blue skirt and a white top. As I sat next to him in the car, I took a deep breath and said, "I'll be fine after I have a margarita." Conan was not an alcoholic, unlike Yusuf.

We headed to Margarita's Mexican Restaurant in Manchester.

I knew all of it was wrong because I was still married, but all I can tell you is that I felt alive for the first time in years. I felt numb going through the motions with Yusuf. My marriage to Yusuf had started to die the moment I realized that alcohol was his true love. With Conan, I felt like I could breathe. I was accepted as I was. Yusuf didn't want me to listen to the music I liked, and he wanted me to wear more African clothes. Yusuf seemed to want to change most things about me, and he definitely didn't like my idea of dying my hair blonde. Conan had been at my local singing competition where I sang Adele songs at Tandy's Bar and Grill; Yusuf had shown no interest in going. Each day that we talked at work, I came to trust Conan more than my own husband, and that told me what I needed to know.

Months later, the rain was pouring on the day I picked up boxes to move out of my first husband's house. Conan came to help bring the boxes to my tan Buick. As he placed the boxes in the trunk, he turned toward me, leaned under my umbrella, and kissed me. I said, "I love you." He softly said, "I love you too."

When Conan kissed me, the world seemed to glow. I felt right in his arms and the stars seemed to glisten above us. I fell hard and fast. And Conan was there to catch me.

HEALING WISDOM

Learning to feel again is so important in learning to trust your intuition. When I began to pay attention to how I felt and why, I was able to make different decisions. Notice how the elements are functioning in your body, just as they function in the Earth.

QUESTIONS FOR REFLECTION

Is your breath steady as a peaceful breeze, or frantic like the whipping wind? Is your personal fire—your energy—extinguished, burning steadily, or a raging blaze? Is your body—your earth, mineral, and water—in balance?

PART TWO

SOUL ROAR

Found Voice

CHAPTER TWENTY

CODA

Coda: *(means "tail" in Italian) a concluding section appended to the end of a work*

At the end of my first marriage, I remember being so miserable that nearly every day I woke up and went to bed with my face soaked in tears.

No one gets married planning to one day get a divorce. I thought love would conquer all. Love did not conquer the fact that we ended up not being right for each other. Even though I chose to leave, it hurt so bad.

On one of the last days at that house in Pembroke, New Hampshire, I was crying, and Yusuf clearly didn't care. He ignored me as I went into the bathroom for the hundredth time to dry my tears. I looked straight into the mirror that day, and I felt my sadness turn into anger. I slowly wiped my tears away and then told my reflection, "I will stop crying today. Today I will make it the LAST day I let him make me miserable."

When I washed the dishes that day, I had Demi Lovato's song "Skyscraper" playing on repeat on my portable Bose speaker.

On the day I finally moved out, Conan and his friend helped me pack up the U-Haul. I packed my car, and I buckled four-year-old Gabriel in the back seat of my car.

"Gabriel, we aren't going to live with your dad anymore."

His little voice sounded calm behind me. "Okay."

As I drove up the hill away from the house, sadness and wonder gripped my heart all at once. All I could think of was my son's little face in the backseat and how nothing would ever be the same again.

I am grateful that, years later after our divorce, the father of my son became sober and is now involved in my son's life. He married a wonderful woman, had a child with her, and is doing well. Gabriel loves his little brother.

HEALING WISDOM

Visualize your ideal self. Imagine yourself as a happy, healthy, fulfilled person. Remember your power. Step on the earth with bare feet to feel its ions that balance your body. Do what makes your heart sing. For me, it was doing yoga, studying astrology, and learning to use angel cards, among other things. Remember your connection to all living things.

QUESTIONS FOR REFLECTION

How would you feel if you trusted yourself enough to achieve your wildest dreams? What is stopping you from feeling that way now?

CHAPTER TWENTY-ONE

IMPRESSIONISM

Impressionism: *a modern French musical style based on blurred effects, beautiful tone colors and fluid rhythms (promoted by Debussy around the turn of the 1900s)*

In a former jail cell, now a Mexican restaurant, Conan asked me to be his wife.

Conan, his kids Greg and Ginger, my son Gabriel, and I all sat together at a table in the restaurant. Conan handed me a rose, which I thought was for my birthday the following day.

I noticed he had three bracelets on his wrist, which seemed strange to me. Just as I was about to ask him about them, he began handing a bracelet to each of the kids. Then he began talking to me about how special I am to him and each of the kids. I was stunned as he pulled out a diamond and emerald ring and asked me to marry him. We took a picture of each of us with our hands on top of each other's and the rose nearby. I wore the ring on my finger and a happiness so bright that I couldn't imagine it would ever be dimmed.

HEALING WISDOM

In my late 30s, I started to realize that I am worthy of ALL love, ALL kindness, and ALL abundance. Nearly 40 years after my birth, I discovered I am already enough—just exactly as I am. My worth is not based on what I do, or where I go, or the brand of anything I own. I am a Divine being, in my belief born from Source, living this human experience. I have had visions of myself inside a crystal cave upon a throne. Later, I read a very similar description of the vision I had received; someone else had seen the same thing. We have forgotten that we are spiritual royalty.

QUESTIONS FOR REFLECTION

How often do you treasure yourself? How often do you reflect on the fact that no one else is quite like you? Do you think the stars in the sky would be as beautiful if only one of them shone?

CHAPTER TWENTY-TWO

VIOLIN

> **Violin:** *a stringed musical instrument of treble pitch,*
> *played with a horsehair bow*

THE BABY THAT COULD HAVE BEEN

Conan and I married at a beach-side ceremony in Hawaii. When we returned, we celebrated with the kids, friends, and family at our back-yard luau in New Hampshire. Through all the happiness of our marriage, I wanted another baby. I wanted a baby of Conan's and my own. Yet I already knew that he couldn't because of his vasectomy. True or not, he told me that his ex-wife, Mary Jane, had made him get one because she didn't want to take any form of birth control because of how it made her feel.

For a little while, we talked about Conan getting a reverse vasectomy. I was thrilled at the idea of providing a little brother or sister for my son. Gabriel had asked me for a brother or sister for years, and I had always planned to give birth to a second child. Conan and I looked into the cost and found out that insurance didn't cover it. It would be an expensive elective surgery with no guarantee of the results we were looking for.

Many nights, especially when drinking red wine, I would bring up the topic of a baby with Conan. Inevitably, I ended up in tears as I pictured a beautiful little "ours" baby that I knew would not be mine. I felt deeply wounded and resentful as though Mary Jane had taken this opportunity away from me. Yet I loved Conan so much that I didn't want to leave him.

Each time a friend mentioned that they were pregnant or their new baby, I was happy for them, yet privately devastated for myself. I carried the pain mostly in secret. After all, I was lucky enough to give birth to one child and to gain two stepkids. Even though I had these children, being deprived of the choice of having another was a difficult burden to carry.

Eventually, I decided to try to stop being so sad about not having a baby and pushed the feelings away from me. If I am meditating for long enough, I recognize the sadness is still within me. The sadness will always be there. I am choosing to allow it to be. I honor the sadness of the baby that could have been, and I accept myself with love anyway.

HEALING WISDOM

While my sadness about the baby that could have been will always be in my heart, I honor that not everything works out the way I plan in life. I use the Emotional Freedom Technique (EFT), also known as tapping, to honor myself and my emotions. Tapping, according to healthline.com, is an "alternative acupressure therapy treatment used to restore balance to your disrupted energy." When I tap, I am essentially clearing out beliefs that don't serve me and making room for beliefs that do. I am still worthy of love, even though I could not have another baby.

QUESTIONS FOR REFLECTION

If you have tried tapping, what have the results been for you? If you have tried other ways of honoring your sadness, what are they? What creative project would you like to give birth to?

CHAPTER TWENTY-THREE

SERENADE

Serenade: *(genre) a Classic instrumental chamber work similar to a small-scale symphony; usually performed for social entertainment of the upper classes*

Although I never gave birth to the daughter I wanted, my stepdaughter, Ginger, became my daughter, born through my heart. My stepson, Greg, is very special to me too.

I met Ginger and Greg when she was four and he was ten. Even before we started dating, Conan wanted to see how I would act with a casual encounter with his kids. He invited me to meet his kids at the beach at the beginning of August 2012. I brought Gabriel with me.

I knew that Ginger was special as soon as I met her because she insisted on covering my legs with seaweed. I laughed and let her place the seaweed on me, unphased by her boldness. As she was heaping the seaweed onto my legs, a seagull swooped in and grabbed her uneaten sandwich next to her. She became outraged, and that was when I saw how brightly her spirit burned. She could be a bright, loving child—or she could be hellfire.

Because I met Greg when he was a bit older, and he was very loyal to his mother, he remained a bit distant with me.

Although it took five years for Ginger to like me because of what she was being told by her mother, when she finally did begin to like me, we became close. She sometimes called me "Mommy," although I made it very clear I would never replace her mother. At first, if Ginger bad-mouthed her mom, I defended her. Then eventually, I just listened quietly and said, "I'm sorry she treats you that way."

I started documenting and reporting their mother's abuse in July 2017, although a police report from February 2017 and my own memory document the abuse of my stepchildren before then. Their mother, Mary Jane, mostly preferred verbal abuse, although sometimes her rage would cause her to slap the kids around. One time, Greg told me she threw a lamp at him. Mary Jane was pale with many freckles and wore her tightly curled black hair pinned back in a bun. She wore wire-rimmed glasses and a perpetual frown. Mary Jane liked to work at local New Hampshire farms that sold produce at farmers markets, and she had rough worker hands. I found it interesting that she, like my dad, enjoyed farming. I often saw her when I visited the local farmers market on Saturdays, and she always scowled at or ignored me.

Without fail, she would target Ginger with her abuse and then send long emails or texts to my husband calling him names. Her favorite name for my husband was "Conan the Moron." Sometimes she called Ginger "Little Conan the Moron." In text messages and emails to Conan (but never to my face), she called me anything that started with R but was not Rachel. For example, Revgel, Riggles, or Ragu. She also had nicknames for my son that were anything but his actual name.

Each time I heard a story of Greg and Ginger's abuse, a story of horror, I was triggered by the memory of my father standing over me screaming. I felt the tightness in my throat and the fear constricting my chest. I could see his blazing brown eyes in my mind's eye. Each word of rage in her text messages or emails to my husband felt like my dad contacting me from the past. I had moved 2,000 miles away from him, but here I was with her. To me, they could both be terrifying; they both spewed anger and hatred. And here I was, married to Mary Jane's ex-husband. Even though they were divorced, she maintained an invisible cord to my husband. She did not want him to be married to her, but she did not want him to be married to anyone else. Her attempts to control him fed her control addiction.

I asked my husband if she had always been this way and what had happened to her. He explained that she had childhood trauma. He said that, at the beginning of their relationship, she was fun and the life of the party. Then, after she had children, he began to see a different side of her. Her childhood trauma caused a deep sickness in her. Although I'm sure her friends and family saw the kind side of her, I didn't experience it.

The year 2017 was also the year that Greg told my husband he wanted to move in with us full-time. With a sense of relief, I contacted my attorney friend who previously worked for child protective services. I asked her to take the case and attended each meeting with her and my husband to prepare for court. During this time, I felt like I was under a kind of psychic attack from Mary Jane. I hired a shamanic healer and told him of my plight. I contributed to the attorney's legal fees, and I went through the healing ceremony. I thought everything was on track. And then Mary Jane badgered Greg until he was guilted into changing his mind about wanting to live with us full-time. Greg wanted full-time, but she convinced him that 50/50 custody was in his best interest. Greg gave in, and then so did my husband because it felt like the easier thing to do. After all, Mary Jane intimidated our attorney. In January 2018, my stepchildren began to live with us half of the time.

So much happened in those three years. Mary Jane withheld multiple visits to our house, otherwise known as parental alienation. She would not allow Ginger and Greg to attend my husband's family funerals. She did not allow Ginger and Greg to go to my son's birthday party because they had to "have a traditional Sunday breakfast." She threw Ginger's new soccer shoes and shorts into the trash and left the trash bag on the side of the road in the rain on the day of her game. Mary Jane slapped Ginger's face because she couldn't find her gloves. Many other problems arose and were communicated through Ginger, Greg, and long, scathing emails and text wars with my husband.

I often knew I had reached my limit when I felt pain and exhaustion in my body. For years, I didn't know what to do unless I was consulting with a counselor or spiritual healer. I had yet to learn to trust myself.

HEALING WISDOM

When you are stressed, ritual can bring a sense of peace into your being. Choose any or all of the following to step into serenity:

Light a candle with reverence. Rub essential oils on your candle or your wrists. Take a salt bath. Say a prayer. Go to counseling. Get creative with your art, your music, or however you would like to express yourself in a way that brings you joy. Meditate. When you breathe in, imagine the breath is coming up from the earth and out through the crown of your head. And vice versa, let the angelic realm fill you with golden breath from above and let it flow down through your body into the earth. Listen to beautiful music. Hold crystals to ground yourself. Place crystals in your bath. Lay on your bed and cover your body with crystals.

QUESTIONS FOR REFLECTION

How do you know when you have reached your limit and need some self-care? What signs can you be aware of to prevent yourself from feeling burned out? What can you do differently next time?

CHAPTER TWENTY-FOUR

ENSEMBLE

Ensemble: *a group of musicians, actors, or dancers who perform together*

In 2013, when Conan and I had been dating for less than a year and my divorce from Yusuf was still in process, I took Conan to my family reunion in Minnesota. He had no idea what to expect and remained very laid-back about everything. His only concern was that, out of spite, Mary Jane wouldn't keep his kids with her while we were gone, which would require us to miss the reunion. Thankfully, she agreed to watch them.

I knew it was true love when my son, then four years old, peed on Conan as he was sleeping while Conan held him in the airport, and Conan didn't break up with me.

When we arrived at the reunion, Conan was stunned that my family voluntarily burst into singing "Hallelujah" at random times. Often, my family members would pray or offer campfires with songs about God. I was raised with amens and hallelujahs being a usual part of the day!

My mother was willing to help pay for my room because she didn't want me staying in the same room as Conan. So she gave me cash to pay for it myself and stood at the table as I instead paid for Conan, Gabriel, and myself to stay in the same room.

During the first night, everyone was on the stage introducing their families and saying a few words about them. They mentioned ages, hobbies, and more.

When it was my turn, I eagerly grabbed the microphone and told the crowded room that Conan was brave for being there. People throughout the room giggled at what I had said, because they knew it was considered scandalous that my divorce wasn't finalized (my divorce took one year) and yet I had brought my boyfriend.

My brother-in-law and my uncle refused to talk to Conan, but my cousin and his wife told us admiringly that they could see how I glowed with Conan by my side. They saw how happy he made me and how happy I made him.

Conan and I had both been through our own traumas and felt safe with each other. We helped each other grow into confident, joyful people who have fun together. We communicate about absolutely everything, whether we are comfortable or not. We ask questions and try our best not to assume, and we sometimes see a marriage counselor. Our open communication and loving patience have saved our marriage despite all of our troubles.

HEALING WISDOM

When a couple of my relatives refused to talk to Conan, I was very hurt. Possibly the most aggravating part of the healing process is the impatience. The emotionally wounded do not heal overnight, and they do not heal in a matter of three years of counseling. This is a process of being willing to fall in love with yourself. If I had loved myself fully, I wouldn't have let their rejection hurt me so much.

QUESTIONS FOR REFLECTION

When you are being rejected, how can you choose to see yourself with love instead? With so much limitless love that exists, can you choose to receive your own and God's/the Universe's love instead of relying on others?

CHAPTER TWENTY-FIVE

FORTE

Forte: *(f) a loud dynamic marking*

Every few years after marrying Conan, I visited North Dakota to see my parents. I brought Gabriel with me on a couple of occasions. Before Gabriel was born, I traveled to North Dakota by myself. While I always felt apprehensive to see my dad, I told myself that we are now adults and will behave like reasonable adults.

One morning when my sisters and I were in town, my dad surprised us by taking us to the local gas station for breakfast. We called the gas station the "C-store" because it was a convenience store. In our small town of 500 people, the C-store was the place for local men to meet and drink coffee together. Families stopped by to get sandwiches or pizza. And that morning, we went to have pancakes.

My dad was in a great mood as he helped all of us sisters with our food. He seemed genuinely happy to see us. I felt like pinching myself to see if this was a dream, and yet half of me still felt mistrustful.

About 15 minutes into our breakfast together, just as I was beginning to relax, my sister Sophie spilled milk on the floor. As she knocked the small carton of milk off the table, the air filled with tension. My dad immediately sprang into action and began yelling in front of everyone. "WATCH WHAT YOU'RE DOING!!!"

I looked down at my lap in embarrassment. Each time he yelled, the memories of my childhood came flooding in. I didn't have much of an appetite for pancakes after that.

HEALING WISDOM

I know, from experiences like this one, that letting go of uncomfortable feelings can be difficult because they are valid. Just as you experience pain more than once in your life, so too do you need to grieve as many times as you need to in order to LET GO. No rules exist for the number of times, or where, or when, or why you let go. Honor your truth. Hold your existence with enough loving reverence that you realize when you are out of alignment with your highest self. Check in with your body, because it has the clues you need. Do you have soreness, stiffness, or feel like you *must* distract yourself with drinking, cleaning, gossiping, or anything other than acknowledging your truth? This is what causes anxiety. When you ignore your feelings and you cover them, your soul is crying out for you to hear.

QUESTIONS FOR REFLECTION

When you are triggered, can you pause for a moment to observe that you are being triggered? What loving thoughts can you offer yourself at these times? How would it feel to calmly respond to an enraged person with a statement as simple as, "It's interesting that you see it that way," and then tactfully speak your truth?

CHAPTER TWENTY-SIX

SHRILL

Shrill: *(of a voice or sound) high-pitched and piercing*

BITTER VALENTINE

On Valentine's Day in 2018, Mary Jane spit at my back as I was walking Gabriel to elementary school. I didn't realize what had happened, but Gabriel told me because he saw it. It was a very cold day, and I had my faux fur-lined hood pulled over my head.

I asked Gabriel, "What did you say?"

"I said, she spit at you."

I stopped in shock, and asked, "Did it hit me???"

"No, it landed near you on the sidewalk." Then Gabriel said something else I couldn't hear very well because of the hood. I felt angry, especially because my child had seen what she did, but I kept walking, thinking just how childish she was being.

Later that day when I picked Gabriel up from school, I had a gnawing feeling that I should ask him about the spitting incident again.

"Gabriel, you told me that Mary Jane spit at me. Then you tried to tell me something else, but I couldn't really hear you with the hood over my head and the wind blowing. What else did you say?"

He looked at me. "I said, she spit at you, then she turned toward me, and she spit at *me*."

My son was nine, nearly ten at the time. I began seeing red. All the possible anger within me rose to the surface. It was one thing for her to spit at my back, but to spit at my nine-year-old child AS HE WATCHED? This was unacceptable.

I took a few deep breaths and began texting my husband immediately. He was at his second job.

"Mary Jane spit at Gabriel and I!" I texted him.

I was so angry. I didn't know what to do. Gabriel had told me the full story at an after-school event at his elementary school. We were there with many parents and kids roaming around. In the distance, I could see my friend who used to work for child protective services and her husband, a police officer. They were at the school with their daughters.

CONFRONTATION

I looked down at my phone and decided exactly what to do. I started a group text with Mary Jane and Conan.

I texted, "Mary Jane, my son told me that he saw you spit at us when I was walking him to school. If you ever spit at or near us again, I will call the police."

Mary Jane responded almost immediately, "Thanks for the paper trail you nut job! If anything, I should be calling the police on you! I'm going to get a restraining order on you like I should have years ago."

It was at that moment that Mary Jane decided this was war, even though I had done nothing but stand up for myself and my son. To Mary, Conan was the enemy, and now so was I and my son.

Don't wait. Involve professionals—counselors, doctors, attorneys, mediators, police (when necessary)—as soon as you can. You are not alone, and you don't need to go through scary or uncertain times by yourself.

On top of Mary Jane's behaviors, I finally had my eyes opened to the fact that after spending so many years solely blaming Mary Jane, my own stepchildren sometimes have toxic behaviors. My own stepkids. I have been in their lives since Greg was ten and Ginger was four. But this awareness was crucial for me in order to examine my stress, my patterns of behavior, and why I often carry so much physical pain in my shoulders and neck. I had to realize why the pain was often so great that it seemed more than I could carry.

I love Ginger and Greg. I want nothing but the best for them. Unfortunately, whether they knew it or not, sometimes their unhealthy behaviors caused me a high level of stress. On several occasions, they stole cash from my purse and quarters from our change jar. They stole some of Conan's and my alcohol. Greg smoked weed in his room, even after we asked him to stop. Their poor choices became a burden that I took onto myself because I thought it was a way to show them love and help them.

I am grateful I am here for Ginger and Greg. I will always love them. But the question became, *How much do I love myself?* When I think of how I have allowed them to drag my energy down, I begin crying. I start feeling so very sorry for Ginger and Greg that they have not been raised by a mother who taught them how to love properly. They are like the "sea pirates" that Buddhist Thich Nhat Hanh described as never knowing how to love. Hanh said that perhaps if he had been raised without being shown how to love, maybe he would have ended up as a pirate too. This was a truth that struck a deep chord with me.

Ginger and Greg have their father, my husband, who did his best to teach them how to love. He tried his absolute best and was often overridden by Mary Jane. Mary Jane was not taught how to properly love. She was left to her own devices from a young age. And because Mary Jane didn't have the loving guidance and was left to run wild, how could the traumatized little girl who never grew up and didn't know how to raise herself, then raise children in a loving way? She didn't know how.

While I have compassion for Mary Jane, Ginger, and Greg, I had to ask myself, *Where was the compassion for myself?*

HEALING WISDOM

It's okay to feel emotion. It's okay to admit when you are not okay.

QUESTION FOR REFLECTION

Where is the compassion for yourself?

You are not to blame for others' poorly chosen behaviors. What lies are you telling yourself? Examine these through meditation and choose to see yourself with love instead.

CHAPTER TWENTY-SEVEN

CRESCENDO

Crescendo: *gradually getting louder*

Perhaps Mary Jane began spiraling when she wanted Ginger tested for ADHD and my husband disagreed. This prompted her to show up in front of our house screaming and honking the horn of her Subaru Outback. Or perhaps when my husband stopped paying her alimony, that was her turning point to ramping up her rage. Either way, Ginger was treated worse and worse with each day that passed, and she began to react to her mother.

In February 2020, I met with Mary Jane for coffee.

At True Brew, I thanked Mary Jane for meeting with me. I said, "As I emailed you, I wanted to meet with you to discuss my needs, your needs, and to ask how we can make supporting Greg and Ginger easier." I proceeded to read aloud the statements about my needs from my notebook. Then I asked what her needs were and offered to have a dialogue.

Mary Jane said, "Well, clearly this meeting is about you and not about my needs. I understand what you are saying, but we can't forget about how you have made my life a living hell."

I repeated, "I have made your life a living hell?" in surprise. I asked, "How have I made your life a living hell?"

She said, "Well, first, there is the spitting incident. If you had bothered to ask me questions about that, you would have found out the truth. Gabriel is always with you. How would he not be with you?"

I said, "When Gabriel told me what happened, Mama bear came out. I think if the same situation happened with you and Ginger, you may have reacted the same way. You and I have different versions of the story. Do you want to hear my version?"

She said, "No, I do not! You called child protective services on me! You and Conan did it together. Lynn told me."

I looked at her with no response because I believe she was trying to get a reaction from me.

I said, "Mary, it sounds like you and I have a different version of reality. I'm willing to leave the spitting incident in the past."

She became very angry, lifted her head and shoulders well above mine with her eyes flashing, and snapped aggressively, "But don't you see that it's not in the past, Rachel? This is exactly the kind of passive-aggressive behavior I would expect from you. I can't trust you. You're aligned with Conan."

I said, "I'm not here to talk about Conan. How can we make supporting the kids easier for all of us?"

She said, "You can't, Rachel. The only thing you can do is tell Conan to communicate with me."

"I do. I ask him to talk to you directly."

"I believe you! I believe you, Rachel. The kids tell me you're a better parent than Conan. They say you do a better job."

"Thank you, I take that as a compliment."

"You should! You really should. I'm only here because you're nice to my kids."

I responded, "Is there anything at all that I can do to make things easier?"

She said, "I don't want to go to your property. I don't want you to go to my property. I don't want to communicate with you. I want Conan to transport the kids and to communicate with me directly." Then she asked, "Is there anything else you would like to discuss? It sounds like you got what you wanted."

I smiled and said, "I was able to express my needs to you and that makes me happy. I don't have anything else to discuss."

She then said she was leaving and mumbled something about getting a new kitchen. Then she clinked my mug with hers like a toast and left. A man sitting at the bar nearby said, "I would have told *her* where to go."

And just like that, all hope of working together for the sake of the kids was clearly gone.

A few days later, Ginger told us that her mother told her, "I hope you fucking die. I hate you! I want to put you into foster care."

The stress of knowing how Mary Jane was treating Ginger was exhausting. A couple of times when Conan was going to bring Ginger and Greg to their mother's, Ginger clung to me and cried on my shoulder. She told my husband, "Don't make me go back there!" As her tears flowed onto my shoulder, I held my stepdaughter with deep sadness. I wanted to protect her. And deep down, I wanted to protect the scared little girl that I had been.

I tried to reason with Conan to tell him he should file an ex parte for the safety of the kids. He was concerned about what Mary Jane would say or do. He believed that if he kept them at our house and filed an ex parte, she would call the police or somehow cause a scene at our house. I didn't know what to do.

HEALING WISDOM

Mary Jane gave me the gift of understanding for the first time where the rage of war comes from. My eyes were opened to how some people do not have compassion for others. However, I had to learn to acknowledge the rage and then let it go. I admit I didn't find it easy to let go. One thing that helped me learn to let go was thinking of Mary Jane as an angry little girl stomping her feet.

QUESTIONS FOR REFLECTION

How do you feel when you think of someone you hate as a little child, stomping their feet? Do you think it may be possible that they experienced trauma and deserve compassion too?

CHAPTER TWENTY-EIGHT

STACCATO

Staccato: *short, detached notes*

BLACK LIVES MATTER

One thing that Mary Jane and I had in common was that we both supported the Black Lives Matter (BLM) movement. Separately, we marched in different protests to show our support for the movement. She marched with my stepson Greg, and they carried signs with phrases such as "Silence is Violence."

I became aware that she posted rather regularly on social media about her support of BLM. She often posted about social justice issues. That's why it was so ironic and sad that Mary Jane was so mentally ill that her actions seemed to show lack of care about my son's life. We found out the truth much later. I am recounting what happened regarding my son based on how Ginger described it to me. I will never forget:

Mary Jane convinced Ginger to report a false story about my son raping Ginger when they were seven and eight years old. Mary Jane wrote this detailed story on a piece of paper, including in her concocted tale that the rape happened in springtime each time after they got ice cream. She even described the clothing Ginger was wearing. Mary Jane made Ginger memorize the false story until she could repeat it back to her. Then she told Ginger that if she didn't tell this lie to the professionals, Mary Jane would bring her to a remote field in Maine, drop her off, and leave her there. Mary Jane had already once left Ginger on the side of the road in Manchester, New Hampshire, and this made Ginger believe that Mary Jane would really leave her in Maine. Of course, Ginger didn't want to be dropped off in a field, so she told the lie to her counselor. The counselor reported the lie to the police.

I knew this was an outright lie because Ginger has always been one of the most outspoken girls I have ever known. She has never been shy and has always expressed herself confidently. In fact, she broke my son's arm when they were little. Ginger would have immediately and loudly told us if the allegations about my son had happened.

I was deeply concerned about the false allegations, not only because Gabriel is my son, but because he is biracial and considered Black. If actually charged with rape, my son would live with that haunting him for the rest of his life. According to the National Association for the Advancement of Colored People (NAACP), these statistics are sadly true:

- A Black person is five times more likely to be stopped without just cause than a white person.
- A Black man is twice as likely to be stopped without just cause than a Black woman.
- One out of every three Black boys born today can expect to be sentenced to prison, compared to one out of six Latino boys and one out of 17 white boys.

For my son to heal from the trauma of this false allegation, he must do so as a Black child who is growing up in a country that still wrestles with racism. The consequences of this allegation would be so much greater for him because he is Black, so the stakes were very high. This lie caused the child protective services case to flip from nearly having Ginger live with us full-time, to our communication with her being restricted. Gabriel and I were ordered to have no contact with her. My husband was ordered to have only supervised phone calls. For about three months, especially because Mary Jane then filed an ex parte to obtain full medical decision-making, we had nearly zero information about my stepchildren. All of it was agonizing.

The day Mary Jane filed the ex parte, she showed up unannounced at our house. I was eating breakfast at the dining room table, looking out the window, when I saw her park her car. I jumped up to go to the door, completely nervous because I had no idea what she was doing. As she climbed the stairs to come into our enclosed porch, I closed the door to the inside of the house. She was filming the whole thing on her phone and sending it through to Conan. I said in a panicked voice, "Conan, call the police!"

He froze, unsure of what to do. I said, "Either call the police, or talk to her!"

I desperately wanted to call the police, and I was so upset with myself at that point that I didn't. I kept hoping that Conan would enforce healthy boundaries and keep us safe by calling the police. He didn't call, and I continued to blame myself—even though it was up to Conan to protect us from the mother of his kids.

Conan and I watched the video that Mary Jane later sent, which showed her putting her camera up to the window after the door was closed, and we could hear her say, "They shut the door on my face." It was terrifying because of the last time she had made a scene in front of our house and another time when she kicked a lantern over on our porch.

I remember sitting on the floor of Ginger's bedroom and crying. I was mad about the whole thing and, despite what Ginger had done, I missed her. I raised her since she was four, and I knew what she did was under the influence of her mother.

POLICE INTERROGATION

I felt broken-hearted and tense as a detective in my living room investigated my son. He interviewed Gabriel, and Gabriel almost cried. He could barely speak because he was shocked by what was happening. Gabriel sat in an armchair with his mask covering his mouth due to the pandemic. We all wore masks. The detective sat in my office chair across from Gabriel (my office was in my living room). Yusef sat on the couch next to his chair, Conan sat on the opposite end of the couch closer to me, and I sat on the love seat next to the child protective services worker.

"Tell me what you like about Ginger," the detective said.

Gabriel was so nervous. "Well, nothing lately because she's been so mean to me."

"There's nothing you like about her?" the detective asked. "Come on, you can tell me. What did you do to her? Did you have any inappropriate touching? I won't judge you if you did or didn't. All I need to know is what happened."

"N-no," my son stuttered. "Nothing happened. I didn't do anything."

"Did you sleep in her bed?"

"No," my son said with tears in his eyes.

The detective looked frustrated. "Look, we can do this the really easy way and you can just tell me what happened. Maybe it would be easier if your parents weren't here. Do you want to talk to me alone?"

"I don't know," Gabriel said.

I looked straight at the detective, very upset. "I am normally the first person to believe if someone is saying they are a victim," I said. "But my son is saying he didn't do it because this is all a LIE!"

The detective turned red all the way through to his blonde hair and yelled at me, "I have to take this seriously! This was reported to us from YOUR step-daughter, and we need to find out what happened! I mean, she likes YOU!" He implied that she liked me, but not her biological parents at that moment.

I gripped the edge of the love seat. "And I like her too," I said calmly. "But she has a history lately of saying things that aren't true. She is so outspoken and would have told us this if it actually happened all those years ago. My son didn't do this."

Everyone in the room looked tense. Yusef speculated aloud, "Are you sure it wasn't the mother who made up this story? She spit at our son in the past."

I very firmly looked at the detective and said, "I spent three years report-ing Mary's abuse of Ginger. Nothing happened. Now she tells one lie and you're taking immediate action." I kept thinking, what would have happened if my son were white?

The detective looked questioningly over at the child protective services worker who looked very uncomfortable. Then the detective looked back at me. "Well, since your son isn't telling us what happened, we will probably have to come back another time to talk to him."

"That's fine," I said. "You're welcome to come back to talk to him. We have nothing to hide."

Although the detective and Yusef left, the child protective services worker stayed. He asked me, "Do you mind if I speak to your son alone?"

My first instinct was to say no, but I agreed to let him. Conan and I left to sit on the front porch while we waited for them to have their conversation.

When it was over, the child protective services worker told us that Gabriel did not say anything suspicious. Later, I asked Gabriel what he had been asked.

Gabriel said, "He asked me to say the words penis and vagina. And he asked me if I like to touch them."

AWAKENING

School pictures happened later that week. Gabriel looked miserable in his photo, and I grieved that this had happened to my innocent son. And yet, I now knew from personal experience that Black boys in the United States simply do not feel safe when police are involved.

I truly loved my husband and my stepchildren, and I did not want this for us. I thought, *If I do enough good things, it will change my situation.* I thought, *If I am just perfect enough, my reality will improve.* And I thought, *If I am peaceful enough, life will become peaceful.* The law of attraction, right? Focus on the good and it will come?

The year 2020 was, as it was for most humans on the planet, a year of CLEAR vision. It was a year of awakening. No longer was I given the option of fantasizing a different reality without action. I no longer had the option of ignoring or hiding from my truth. Or anyone's truth, really. No matter how positive I was, Mary Jane lurked angrily in my husband's emails, text messages, and stressed-out stories from my stepkids. Every time the phone rang, we tensed in anticipation that it was her in a rage. Every time a vehicle that looked like hers drove past, we held our breath thinking it could be her.

I couldn't paint sparkles over this revolting reality.

HEALING WISDOM

As my anger rose over what was happening, my body began to suffer more. I discovered that the right side of the body is masculine, and the left side is feminine. I learned to notice where I have tension or pain in my body. If you are feeling that you have trouble with manifesting your goals into reality, your best bet is to meditate on where your imbalance may be. Sit in silence with your eyes closed and ask your body what it needs. Accept and allow that you have pain instead of fighting against it.

QUESTIONS FOR REFLECTION

When you fight against how your body is, how do you feel? When you accept it as it is with love, how do you feel? How can you choose to see your body and your suffering differently?

CHAPTER TWENTY-NINE

FORTISSIMO

Fortissimo: *(f) a very loud dynamic marking*

IT GETS WORSE

In May 2020, we were deeper into the pandemic. Tensions between Mary Jane's household and ours continued to increase. After consulting a medium named Amy Major (who is able to converse with spirits) and using my own observation of Ginger's change in voice, aggressive behavior, and sour demeanor, I found out that on May 10th, Ginger went hiking and had spirits attach themselves to her. This was essentially a possession. Amy shared with me that two aggressive male spirits had attached themselves to Ginger, and this was not the first time they had possessed someone. She said that, in fact, they enjoyed it. Ginger began to paint her face in a very dark way with lots of black eyeliner, somewhat like a clown. She painted her face this way nearly every day. I paid for Amy to remove the two male spirits from Ginger and thought this would be the last I would need to worry about this spiritual problem.

For two days after that day in May, Mary Jane withheld the kids' visits to our house. She told Greg and Ginger they were not allowed to come to our house until they spoke to counselors. We were confused why she was acting this way, but it was not the first time. Mary Jane had withheld many visits over the years.

On June 7th, Ginger revealed to Conan and me that when she was playing with her little brother Eddie and crossing his arms across his body, Mary Jane began to yell at her. Mary Jane made Eddie go inside the house, then slapped Ginger on the face four times. Ginger tried to push her away and Mary Jane pushed back. Her mom said, "You wanna go???" as she towered over Ginger.

Suddenly, Ginger's grandmother arrived, and Mary Jane left her alone. When Ginger recounted the story to us, she told us, "I want to kill myself and never see my mom again!"

We were very concerned, but Ginger did not yet have a plan that we knew of to kill herself.

Then on June 18th, 2020, when Mary Jane was driving Ginger to a friend's house, she became angry that Ginger didn't know the directions for getting to the house. Mary Jane pulled the top of Ginger's hair four times and then made her get out of the car on the side of the highway. Mary Jane drove her car away and LEFT her 12-year-old daughter on the side of the busy interstate for ten minutes.

When we found out about what happened, my husband and I immediately called child protective services. At this point, the child protective worker was about to place Ginger with Conan and me full-time. But just when we thought this might be a possibility, the unthinkable happened.

A SHOCKING DEVELOPMENT FOR GINGER

On June 30th, 2020, our family changed forever. I was helping my son Gabriel with the dishes when our doorbell rang. My husband answered the door at the other end of our house and found a police officer standing there. The officer shared that the police department had received a call from one of Ginger's friends expressing concern that she was suicidal. With concern,

Conan told the police that he had dropped Ginger off at her mother's house half an hour prior.

The police officer drove to Mary Jane's house. After he left, Mary Jane immediately called my husband to scream at him. She yelled, "Why didn't you tell me that a police officer was coming to my house?!"

Honestly, we knew she would be upset either way, and the less time we had to hear her yelling, the better.

On the morning of July 1st, Mary Jane took Ginger to Riverbend for a psych evaluation. Mary Jane called my husband for insurance information. When Conan tried to ask her what was happening, she hung up on him. We had zero information until Conan had the idea to call Concord Hospital that night. The nurse who spoke to him seemed to behave strangely. She seemed hesitant to even share that Ginger was there.

Four days later, we found out that my husband could only have supervised phone calls with Ginger. We were stunned to learn that Gabriel and I were ordered to have no contact with Ginger. Yet we had no idea why.

I was beside myself. My husband was devastated, and we were both so confused. What was happening??? I got into my car, feeling a rage building in me that needed to go somewhere. I drove onto the highway and began screaming and crying. I was SO VERY ANGRY. For so long, I felt like I had worked hard to preserve my family despite the chaos from my step kids' mother. I couldn't help but feel that she had dropped a bomb onto our family.

For all of July and August, I did not see Ginger or Greg. Conan saw Ginger a couple of times at the hospital with special permission. Several times, I sat on her bedroom floor and cried for her. I missed her so much. I whispered into the air, "I just want my girl to come home."

RETURN

In August 2020, Ginger left the hospital and went back to her mother's home. On August 18th, I received a frantic voicemail from one of Mary Jane's neighbors. The neighbor sent me videos and photos showing Mary Jane towering over Ginger and pushing and pulling her. He said, "Oh my god, you have to call me right now!"

By the time I heard the message, Mary Jane's neighbor Steve had called my husband already. According to Steve, Ginger was strangled, slammed into a car, and punched. Later, we found out that at the time the police arrived, Ginger had marijuana in her system. Her mom had allowed her to drink alcohol and smoke weed at age 12, and possibly before then.

The last week of August, Ginger stayed with our friend Serena because the police were not yet done investigating my son. It was during this time the Department of Children, Youth, and Families (DCYF) wanted to place Ginger with us half the time, and with her mother the other half of the time. I was LIVID.

I thought, *HOW can someone with a criminal history and years of documented abuse be awarded half custody?* Conan and I worked HARD all our lives, and we have never been arrested. Yet DCYF wanted to place Ginger back with her mother half of the time. I COULD NOT HANDLE MY LEVEL OF ANGER. Conan and I have ALWAYS followed the law, served others, and chosen good things for other people. We were being told that Becket Family Services would figure it out, but it would likely be a 50/50 living situation for Ginger, for after all, they said they had no reason to remove her from her mother's home. This was not abuse and neglect according to them—EVEN THOUGH THE POLICE REPORT SHOWED PHOTOS OF THE MARKS OF HER MOTHER'S FINGERS ON GINGER'S NECK. Another photo in the police report showed Mary Jane holding out her open palms for inspection.

Meanwhile, Greg wasn't responding to text messages, phone calls, or emails.

GINGER STRUGGLES

I was nervous and unsure of what to expect when Conan and I went to pick up Ginger from our friend Serena's house. As Conan and I were driving to Serena's to pick Ginger up, Greg showed up at our house where Gabriel was alone. Greg angrily grabbed his things and moved out, barely talking to Gabriel. He left his house key on his dresser for us to later find with sorrow.

On September 1st, 2020, I saw Ginger with a demon or other attachment in her. Her voice was raspy, almost like Gollum from *The Hobbit*.

She wanted to play basketball because she played it a lot in the hospital. In front of Serena, Ginger admitted that her mom had coached her to make false allegations about Gabriel. Ginger said, "My mom wrote down a script for me to memorize. She made me repeat it over and over again until I was ready to lie about Gabriel to my counselor." I was horrified, yet not surprised. This was what I suspected had happened.

Ginger was home for four days, during which she punched two holes in her bedroom wall and cut herself. The first day, she tried to run away twice. On September 8th, 2020, I found Ginger on top of the bathroom sink with wild eyes. Her voice was extra raspy and she was very angry. She clutched her bent knees and looked at me with a piercing gaze. "What???" she asked me wrathfully.

"You said you wanted to get your lip pierced. What if, instead, we get your tragus pierced like mine?" I asked, attempting to negotiate based on a conversation we had just had with her dad on the porch.

"NO!" she screamed and then flew off the sink, out of the door, and off to her room. I could hear her punching a second hole into her wall.

That night, Conan tried to talk her down for at least half an hour as I sat on the porch. She was seated on the curb on the corner of the street. Finally, I came outside. Using the flashlight of my phone, I could see blood pouring down her arm. She refused to go with us to the hospital. Conan called the police.

The police swarmed our house. I stood there in the dark in my Zyia blue shorts, tank top, and no bra. At least four police officers and two EMTs checked her. Ginger was so proud and tried to act tough. I cried. She said, "Don't cry, Rachel!" with a smirk. They took her in an ambulance to Concord Hospital where she spent seven days and then transferred to Hampstead Hospital.

Afterward, Conan and I escorted a police officer to Ginger's bedroom where we discovered sharp objects on her bed. She found Greg's pocket knife he had left behind and my scissors that I didn't realize were in the back of my desk. She slashed her arm and cut herself with the edge of a tape dispenser. We had no idea she had these things. As I spoke to the police officer in her bedroom, I couldn't believe what was happening.

On the day that Ginger was scheduled to return from her third and final stay at Hampstead Hospital, I sat in the parking lot of the hospital waiting for my husband to come outside with her. As I waited, I knew I would see Mary Jane at some point. She had to sign the hospital release paperwork too. In the past, I would have smiled at Mary Jane and hoped that maybe she would smile back too. At that moment, I was long past ever smiling at Ginger and Greg's mom ever again. I was so angry at her for what she had done to the children, and to my own husband when they were married. Her abusive, toxic ways were all too reminiscent of how my father had been at times. Except she seemed even more cold-hearted.

SAFETY FIRST

Initially, DCYF asked me to have Gabriel start living with his father at least half-time or full-time. I felt that I was essentially being asked to choose between my son and my stepdaughter because they didn't yet know the outcome of Gabriel's investigation. This choice hurt my heart more than anything.

At first, I almost said yes to Gabriel living with his father half of the time. But the truth is, with the exception of soccer transportation, I have done the majority of everything for Gabriel. I didn't feel comfortable with this choice. I pushed back with DCYF and said that Gabriel is staying with me. I have had primary custody of him since he was four years old.

As a result of Gabriel's staying and Ginger's at-risk behavior, Conan and I had to agree to a safety checklist with DCYF. In our house, Conan removed Ginger's door. We installed cameras everywhere except for the bathroom and had an alarm installed on Gabriel's door. We locked up the alcohol and placed all sharp objects into a lockbox to prevent Ginger from cutting herself. Conan and I had to sign a document stating that all of these things were done and submit to a home inspection by DCYF before they would allow Ginger to come back to live with us.

In early September 2020, Ginger returned to our house full-time. One of the most exhausting pieces of Ginger's return was that five new professionals were in our home or on Zoom nearly every day of the week. Ginger had appointments with Becket Family Services, child protective services, her psychiatrist, and two counselors.

Unless someone has experienced five professionals coming into their home each week while they are trying to work full-time and the children are attempting to do remote learning full-time—all in a one-level apartment— the immense pressure we were under is hard to fathom. For one thing, even though we had locked all known sharps away in a lock box, Ginger was constantly at risk of finding things with which to cut herself. She became an expert at breaking paperclips in half and pulling nails out of the wall simply to obtain a sharp object.

I would also sometimes have to leave in the middle of a Zoom committee meeting because DCYF needed to meet with my husband and me about the ongoing care of my stepchild. And, when I was in the middle of big projects for work, I would need to stop and participate in family-building exercises with a social worker. Though these were clearly designed to have Mary Jane and Conan co-parent more effectively, co-parenting is not an option for a biological mother who gaslights and projects. Parallel parenting is the only option in this case.

One night, as I was sitting comfortably on the couch in the living room next to Ginger as we watched the TV show *Criminal Minds*, the detective who had questioned Gabriel about the false rape accusation knocked on our door. He came into our house with another police officer and looked right at me.

I looked at him with an expression that acknowledged him and made me feel victorious. I looked back at the TV screen as my husband talked to him.

My husband asked the detective, "What is this about?"

The detective said, "As you know, Ginger has been accused of hitting her mother with a broom. We are also charging her with punching two holes in her bedroom wall since it is not her property."

Yes, although Ginger defended her mother's abuse with a broom, she was the one being sent to court for a potential simple assault while her mother was charged with nothing. Thankfully, Ginger's charge was closed due to good behavior.

Another issue is that at least two of the professionals texted me about Ginger on a daily basis. It was exhausting keeping up with their questions. While my husband coordinated some things for Ginger, I was also busy coordinating for her. I ended up contacting the National Alliance on Mental Illness (NAMI) to find someone to talk to and text for *my* support.

Sometimes, when one of Ginger's counselors came to meet with her, I went on a long walk. Her suffering was hard on me. I began to strongly feel the need to care for myself more than ever before. The weight was so heavy on my shoulders, and I was so tired. I took baths nearly every night. Everything I did felt like I was doing it in slow motion because it was so much at once. And yet, I loved Ginger so much that it was never an option for me not to do what I did.

SPIRITUAL HEALING

In October 2020, after Ginger had been home for about a week, I decided I couldn't allow whatever attachment or demon that I believed was causing Ginger to behave so aggressively to live in our home any longer. I felt a personal responsibility as a spiritually awakened being who was aware of this negative attachment or demon living in Ginger. I had seen such a huge change in her that I thought was all due to some other entity within her. When I would attempt to do anything to cleanse our house of negative energy, such as burning sage, Ginger would always quickly leave the room. She was on edge, despite her medication, and brimming with rage. Looking back, I think that yes, something of a negative spiritual event had occurred; and also, the trauma from Ginger's mother strangling her had changed her.

I had enough of this feeling of needing to sage my house so often, and I decided to go to a local spiritual store that sold crystals and other metaphysical items. The owner had told me that if I brought Ginger with me on that day, a man would be available to perform an exorcism for her. I was nervous and unsure of what to expect, but I felt very strongly that this was the only solution for our household. Ginger, her romantic girlfriend Cadence, and I drove in my red Mazda3 to the store. After we parked, we put our pandemic masks on and walked up the stairs of the brown building that housed a hair salon and metaphysical store.

As soon as we walked through the doors, I felt the energy of the entire building shift. The owner spotted me immediately. A couple of other people who worked at the store looked at us with wide eyes as I introduced Ginger and Cadence, as if they had been talking about us before we came to the store. The owner swallowed deeply, quickly gathered herself to look calm, and told me that Jerome would be with us in a few minutes.

"Jerome is doing a spirit gallery. He should be out in about ten minutes, and he'll let you know when he's ready for you."

"Thank you," I said.

We examined different crystals, pendants, and angel card decks as we waited. My nervous energy was building as my mind flashed to movie scenes I had seen of exorcisms. *Was Ginger's body going to convulse?* I wondered. I imagined her perching on the ceiling as I had found her perched on our bathroom sink. With my eyes closed, I shook my head to shake the image from my mind. I was determined to go through with this process for our family's sake.

Finally, the small group of women who had been in the spirit gallery began leaving the back room. They exited the white door into the main part of the store and chatted with each other. They seemed very content and wandered to the front of the store. Jerome didn't come out for a little while longer. The owner told us that he was preparing the room for our session.

I looked at Ginger. "How are you doing?"

"Fine," she said calmly. She seemed unphased by what we were doing. She seemed ready. "Look at this!"

Ginger held up a small crystal pyramid with four points sticking out of each side. They were amethyst and other stones.

One of the employees at the store told us, "If you hold that up to your throat, the energy is crazy!"

Ginger tried it. "Whoa, that's true!"

"I want to try it," I said. I held the crystal pyramid up to my throat and instantly felt a gathering of energy at my throat. Before I could have any kind of reaction, Jerome interrupted us.

EXORCISM

"Hello," he said with a very deep, calm voice.

"Hi, I'm Rachel. This is Ginger and her girlfriend Cadence. They've been dating for a few months."

"Come in," he beckoned us.

Jerome shook Ginger's hand and brought her to a red leather chair. Cadence and I sat about ten feet behind her on zero gravity chairs. Being in

Jerome's presence instantly calmed me. He was confident and spoke with a warm, steady voice.

The owner of the store asked if we needed anything, and after I said no, she closed the door to give us privacy. Jerome stood in front of Ginger, planted his feet firmly on the ground, and raised his arms. He began quietly with what sounded like a prayer, then became louder as he addressed the attachment in Ginger.

"Elizabeth," he said kindly. "It's okay, your time being with Ginger is over. You can still communicate with Ginger whenever you would like." The air shifted to feel like a question mark. I couldn't see this entity, but I could feel its presence.

"Elizabeth, I know you can hear me. Do you see the light at the back of the room? My mother is over there. She helps spirits cross over. She is in Heaven waiting for you. If you go to her, she will bring you safely to the other side." He motioned his hands in front of Ginger's body as if coaxing the spirit to move. His voice was reassuring.

The entire experience was calming. I trusted Jerome's work without fear. He was confident and exuded care for Ginger from what I could tell under his pandemic mask. The exorcism didn't seem strange, and it was very real. I felt happy as I saw Ginger slowly being freed from the entity. I couldn't physically see any kind of spirit, but I could sense what was happening.

"Yes, good," Jerome said. "Keep going, Elizabeth. It's okay. You can let go. You can still visit Ginger, but it will be different than you're used to. Now go to the light. Yes, that's it. Keep going. You're almost there."

Again, the energy in the room shifted from heavy to light. The air felt more breathable. Ginger lowered her chin down to her chest. And then she shifted, as though her entire body was lighter.

Jerome talked softly to Ginger for a little while. Then Cadence and I rose out of our zero gravity chairs at the back of the room and approached her. Ginger seemed slightly dazed, and yet more calm.

I felt proud—and somewhat strange—to be part of the experience.

Jerome told me, "She will look completely different in six months."

And he was exactly right.

HEALING WISDOM

Although I said this before, it's worth repeating: hire others to help you. You do not need to go through difficult situations alone.

QUESTIONS FOR REFLECTION

How can you delegate tasks to others when you are stressed? Whom can you hire to help make your life easier during difficult times?

CHAPTER THIRTY

GLISSANDO

Glissando: *a rapid slide between two distant pitches*

THE EATING DISORDER

Some time during the summer, Ginger had developed an eating disorder. The exhaustion of professionals always coming into our home, coupled with the sadness of Ginger being added to the waitlist for an eating disorder clinic, was heavy on my shoulders. I just wanted her to be okay, and her struggles to eat enough or at all reminded me of my own overeating as a child. We both have used food as a means of control. Every day felt sad and uncertain. I imagined Christmas without Ginger and I wanted to cry.

During this time, I was also worried about what would happen regarding the investigation into Ginger's false allegations about Gabriel. The detective wouldn't call me back, so I called his boss on October 13th and was able to hear back from the detective that Gabriel's name was being cleared. No charges were pressed, but damage from the lie had already been done.

Greg returned to apologize on January 2nd, 2021. After six months of no contact with him, we found out that his mother had threatened to take away his vehicle if he talked to us.

Each day, the pain in my shoulders and neck felt overwhelming. I was desperate for a way to let it go. During the darkness of winter, the one thing that brought my spark back was returning to nature through a practice called Agnihotra. For years, I have known and benefited from the sound healing services of Carlos Perez. Naturally, when he invited me to join his Back In Motion Explorers Facebook group, I accepted. In that group, I learned about the Vedic tradition of a fire purification ceremony called Agnihotra. At sunrise and sunset each day during the month of February, I participated in the Agnihotra ceremony by watching videos in a social media group. In each video, Carlos and his wife demonstrated the ceremony by burning a sacred fire in an inverted copper pyramid and chanting a beautiful, sacred prayer. The fire, burned on dung coated in ghee and brown rice, purified the air and provided a meditative experience. Agnihotra brought me back to myself during those moments, away from the chaos happening in my family.

In the summer of 2021, we continued to wait for a bed at the eating disorder clinic for Ginger. I gave up on the idea and instead looked for ways we could encourage her to love herself. And for me to treat myself with care.

HEALING PRACTICES

I listened to Gabby Bernstein's *Judgment Detox* audiobook as I went for a walk each morning, and I reflected on how I could remove my judgment of Ginger's mother, Mary Jane. I reflected, prayed, burned sage, moved a selenite wand over my body, and still I felt angry. Each day my body felt pain, and nearly every day I found myself drinking red wine. I drank, and I ate more, and I began to gain back some of the weight I had worked so hard to lose.

Based on my past success with Carlos' healing abilities, I decided that I needed to hire three different spiritual healers. I felt that the three healers could resuscitate me after the trauma of what happened to my family in 2020: my stepdaughter wanting to commit suicide and in a mental health facility three times, her mother coaching her to make a false rape allegation about my son, my stepson disowning my husband and I for six months because he believed whatever his mother said and threatened to take away his car if he talked to us, my stepdaughter developing an eating disorder, Ginger beginning to live with us full-time while having a stream of social workers enter our house each week, my husband having to quit his second job to take care of her...all of this accumulation. I was inclined to run away. But I stayed. I stayed because I love myself, and I love them, and I wanted to learn how to be in peace despite this chaos.

The first healer named Samantha Shea Suprenant, recommended by my colleague Jordan at Heifer International, accessed my *Akashic Records* and performed a soul retrieval. The *Akashic Records* are also known as *The Book of Life* or *God's Book of Remembrance*.

The soul retrieval was to bring back a piece of my soul that had been lost due to stress or trauma. During Samantha's time accessing my *Akashic Records*, she connected with one of my past lives when my name was Elizabeth. Samantha channeled Elizabeth and wrote:

THE GREAT DIVIDE
Although the pages may seem black and white, it is only the line drawn down the middle that causes the great divide. Corners give color, they express our fingertips. DNA, patterns, energy of color, of life, are hidden within treasure. Black and white is merely a block from seeing all that is true, colorful light.

Samantha then sent me on a "Spirit Ship" journey for 40 days. Each day, she sent me meditations and readings to reflect on, sometimes about angels. I journaled and put all my worries and cares into a box. I burned candles and prayed. She performed a distance healing on me and in it, without knowing any of my history, envisioned having to perform CPR on me. She brought me back to life. Her healing ceremony for me caused me to accept compassion for myself; I stopped blocking all forms of compassion. I started to believe it was okay for me to go on, to move forward with finding joy in my life again.

The second healer, Carlos, who introduced me to Agnihotra, performed a sound healing on me. I described my trauma, and he listened with compassion. His eyes widened as I shared how I had discovered that I am a witch despite being raised Christian, how I can hear trees speak to me when I place my hands upon them, and how I knew that my Divine masculinity was rising. I sensed that my body and energy felt crooked, and he said that he could see that I looked crooked. He used biofield tuning forks above my body as I lay on a massage table to soothe and align the energy of my body. He also played musical crystal bowls and a Native American drum. During the session, as he placed the bio-tuning fork below my ribcage, I finally *knew* what happened to me. I could sense that, because I had been so traumatized by what happened, my soul was essentially hiding in four corners of my being, completely off-center. I could see I had been trying to escape in every possible way. I was afraid to center myself again. I took a deep breath and allowed the shaman to do his work. He helped me with the rise and fall of my belly and chest, coaxing me to *breathe*. I felt that I was reborn into an authentic Rachel, and he saw this for me. The old was falling away, and the new was beginning for me like a spiritual baby.

The third healer, Kim LaJoie, became necessary after I was lifting weights and my shoulder collapsed. I learned about her from my Association of Fundraising Professionals (AFP) mentor. Literally and metaphorically, it felt like the weight of the world was no longer sustainable. I could no longer carry this situation or these people on my back. Although Ginger was far more healed compared to half a year before, I had little support during my traumatic time. It wasn't on purpose; it was just the pandemic and the rare times that I saw my friends. On top of that, my family lived so far away.

YOU ARE NOT ALONE

Before I went to see the third healer, I went for a long walk in the woods near Auburn Street in Concord. I veered off the main path and walked further into the woods, eagerly stepping my way toward the tree that I loved to place my hands upon. A gentle breeze stirred old yellow leaves on a smaller, nearly barren tree as though the leaves were waving hello to me. I looked around to be sure no one was watching, then asked the tree, "What is the message you have for me today, for the greatest good?"

I felt through my fingertips that the tree vibrated with life, preparing for spring. I saw the moss and lichen on the tree, and I felt the tree whisper to me, "You are not alone." I thanked the tree, thanked the Universe with a reverent prayer, spent a little more time placing my hands on other trees, then picked up my fitness tracker from a rock where I had laid it. As I picked up the tracker to put it on my wrist, I looked up to see a beautiful golden retriever.

"Hi, puppy!" I exclaimed as this beautiful dog bounded through the trees, brush, twigs, and grass toward me. The dog was in need of a trim. The golden retriever bounded happily toward me and let me pet her. I was surprised as she seemed to come out of nowhere.

Her owner hung back and didn't make eye contact. He lit his cigarette and called the dog, "Come on, Hazel!" Then he headed down a different path as the dog turned and ran over to join him.

When I finally saw the third healer, she worked her magic on my injured shoulder and told me she had a message for me. It was the same message I had received from the tree in the woods: "You are not alone."

As we continued to talk, she told me, "Every year on Saint Patrick's Day, today, something happens to remind me of my golden retriever who passed away."

I woke up in the middle of the night, eyes wide open, remembering the golden retriever I had seen in the woods. I felt very strongly that I was not alone, and I did not need to carry my family's burdens on my own.

HEALING WISDOM

Just as you do not have to handle difficult situations alone physically, you do not have to handle them alone spiritually. You have spiritual beings available for you to call upon—whatever you believe. Although you can't see them, you are supported spiritually too. When I began to trust the Universe, miracles began to happen.

QUESTIONS FOR REFLECTION

What is an area in your life where you can ask for spiritual guidance or support? Have you asked for what you desire? Are you being clear enough when you ask God or the Universe for what you want?

PART THREE

SOUL SONG

Harmony

CHAPTER THIRTY-ONE

HOME KEY

Home key: *the "home" key of a tonal composition*

FULL CUSTODY OF GINGER

Two days before Mother's Day, love won. My husband and I won full custody of Ginger after an intense legal battle. She is safe. The irony was not lost on me. While the softer side of me felt sympathy for Mary Jane and the pain she must have felt, I also understood that she created this situation. This was not something my husband and I had chosen.

We won because we had an amazing attorney, and because all of the professionals wrote in their reports that Ginger should live with us. The judge complimented us for how we were taking care of Ginger's mental health. I wanted to cry with relief when he acknowledged what we had done to save this girl.

I was lying on an acupuncture table when the tears came. I realized that the immense pain under my armpit and on the top of my shoulder was from the burden of responsibility I had placed ON MYSELF for things I did not do.

I placed my hand on my sad, tight, nearly collapsed lungs. I closed my eyes in deep sadness and did the following:

I moved my hand to my heart to bring myself back to the present moment. I told myself

gently with tender compassion, "I see you. I see what happened to you. It wasn't your fault. I love you. Thank you. I'm sorry. Please forgive me."

I did not harm Ginger. I did not make Greg stop talking to me. I did not cause Gabriel to be investigated by the police. I did not make my husband's life miserable with long, scathing, harassing emails, text messages, and voicemails.

Mary Jane did these things. Yet I had placed them on my shoulders, and it felt like my shoulders were beginning to freeze and break off.

This realization of truly looking at what I was telling myself and subconsciously believing was life-changing.

I did not make my dad strangle me. It was not my fault. And yet it took until I was nearly 40 years old to tell my younger self, "Beautiful young girl, I see you. It was not your fault what happened to you. And you should be very proud that you lived through it all and are now telling your story. I'm proud of you for using your voice, which you silenced for so long."

I realized that when I was unable to see my self-worth, the lies others told me and the lies I told myself were lies that I believed. I took these lies in and let my heart soak in them. I walked around with a heart flooded with sorrow and bitterness, believing that only the lucky girls could be pretty. I thought it was my destiny to be overweight, to be rejected, to have greasy, unkempt hair, to look as ugly as I felt. I thought, *Why shouldn't I give up on myself since so many other people have?* And now I know that giving up is not an option for me.

Place your hand over your heart, close your eyes, take a deep breath and say, "It is safe to be in my body. It is safe for me to be here. It is safe for me to live on this planet. It is safe to be me."

HEALING WISDOM

Stop blaming yourself for that which you did not create.

QUESTIONS FOR REFLECTION

What do you blame yourself for? When you blame yourself for something you didn't do, how can you forgive yourself for feeling this way? What thoughts can you choose instead?

CHAPTER THIRTY-TWO

HARMONY

Harmony: *the combination of simultaneously sounded musical notes to produce chords and chord progressions having a pleasing effect*

SAFE TO BE ME

Now that the trauma is behind me, I allow myself to be in my body. Each morning, despite my anxiety, I choose to practice peace by meditating. As I meditate each morning, I whisper "thank you" to the Universe. Great Spirit, Divine Goddess: Thank you, thank you, thank you. I am safe.

Each day is a new chance to start over and choose peace again—sometimes hour by hour. Life is still not perfect. Ginger sometimes struggles with her anger, lack of eating, vaping, cutting, and making poor choices, and Conan and I are left to pick up the pieces. I find self-care and boundaries invaluable in these situations. I believe a brighter day is ahead for Ginger. That is up to her.

Greg remains distant from Conan and I, although we see him once in a while. I dream of the day he does not feel he needs to choose between his mom's household and dad's household. And yet, if that doesn't happen, I love and accept myself anyway.

Gabriel is not the happy-go-lucky kid he used to be. He is doing his best to be a normal teenager despite what happened to him. Yet I, like many other awakened souls, now understand the practice of being at peace despite chaos outside. I am aware of the challenges and love myself enough to choose my peace.

I am open to my intuition, and I am guided. The heavens, Earth, and all the unseen beings of love support me. I am not alone. And my journey of my rebirth into the woman I have always been meant to be is now. As I place my hand on my heart, I am home. I am ready each day to speak my truth. I wish the same for you.

Although I grew up Christian, witchcraft became part of my healing journey. I know that certain people in my life will disown me for saying this, but this is my truth. I work with magic of the light, not of the dark. I respect the lessons that dark experiences have taught me. I personally have no interest in dark magic, although I know others who use it. In Christianity, you are generally taught that all magic or witchcraft is evil. This is misleading, as every religion and belief has the possibility of being used as a tool of the light or the dark. Each human has both darkness and light in them, and this choice exists—even in Christianity.

When I cast spells of protection or for manifestation, they work. When I connect to the earth through ritual, I feel myself heal and transform. Layers of ancestral karma and pain were stripped away through my practice of witchcraft. I discovered the power that had lain dormant in me for lifetimes. I came to realize, although I was raised to believe it was taboo, that I am a medium, a healer, an alchemist, a witch, and a medical intuitive. I can see things and people and know things about them without being told any information. I am a singer, a poet, and a writer inspired by the Divine. I view my creations as a spiritual act.

I realize my ways are not for everyone, and not everyone else's ways may be for me. I write to tell you that I have the great privilege of being raised one way and believing a different way as an adult. To experience and see both perspectives is a genuinely important gift because it means I can see the world with both eyes open. I was raised a Republican, then became a Democrat;

now I am more of an Independent. I was raised homophobic, and yet knew I was bisexual since age 12. I am now a member of Parents, Family, and Friends of Lesbians and Gays (PFLAG), supporting the LGBTQ+ community. I am proud to be who I am today, and I sing anyway. I recognize that my painful experiences that I have overcome have made me stronger. I now wear my experiences as a badge of honor.

HEALING WISDOM

Give thanks to the earth below, not only God or the Universe above. If you send your thanks below, above, and all around, your gratitude will keep you grounded. Be thankful for this present moment. You are here now.

QUESTIONS FOR REFLECTION

How can you shift your perspective from victim to victor? How have you been victorious over situations in your life? What song can you sing to celebrate that you have overcome?

$($ CONCLUSION $)$

OUTRO

Outro: *the concluding section of a piece of music or a radio or television program*

A NEW DAWN

"We thought of life by analogy with a journey, of a pilgrimage that had a serious purpose at the end. The thing was to get to that end. Success, or whatever it is, maybe Heaven after you're dead. But we missed the point the whole way along. It was a musical thing, and we were supposed to sing, or to dance, while the music was being played."

– Alan Watts

Right before Father's Day in 2021, I finally had the opportunity to fly back to North Dakota to see my family. My sister Josie and my brother Brandon were planning to be in Zeeland, and my sister Sophie already lived there. I thought, why not join them?

Immediately, I planned to do a ceremony on the earth while visiting my family's farm. I wanted to place my hands on the earth and feel her energy. I wanted to make peace with my past.

Before I flew out to see my family, I contacted Jeanita Kennedy, a Native American healer from the Diné (Navajo) Nation who was living in North Dakota. I had met her through social media after my sister Sophie connected us through a group about spirituality.

"Jeanita," I messaged her, "I want to do a sacred ritual on the land of my family's farm. I want to send healing energy to the land that used to be Native American land. How can I respectfully do this?"

She made it clear that if my intention was pure and I brought an offering of fruit and tobacco, the ritual would show respect. I became increasingly excited as she continued.

Jeanita replied, "When it comes from heart-centeredness, it's always appreciated. Your heart and why you are doing it, they already know. The spirits are waiting there for you. If you can, do it before the sun comes up." She added, "There will be a lot of women spirits there. And you will feel them embracing you with love and thanks, taking you in as one of their own."

I thanked Jeanita profusely and began my mental checklist with eagerness. I offered to send her a donation, and when she declined, I sent a gift to the Standing Rock Reservation. This was how I began to send my gratitude to the land even before arriving.

When I arrived at the Bismarck airport, picked up my luggage, and walked out the sliding doors, I was surprised to see my dad standing right there. I was overcome, although I maintained my composure. I hadn't expected him to be there. I hugged him, and he hugged me back. I felt so surprised that he seemed happy to see me.

I noticed during this visit that it was different from all of my other visits, and that was because I saw my parents differently. My mom got out of the van and came over to hug me too. I began to see them with more mature eyes and with a compassionate heart that understood they didn't know any better. As they raised me, they had done what they thought was best at the time, even though child abuse is never okay. I do not excuse their behavior, nor do I condone it. What my dad did and what my mom allowed was completely unacceptable.

And yet, my heart opened to consider their suffering too. Perhaps my dad had an undiagnosed mental health issue. I am not licensed to diagnose, but I wondered if he is bipolar or is on the spectrum. And I wondered how living with someone like him would affect someone like my mother and her reasons for making certain decisions.

When I opened my eyes to see my parents this way, I had so much more patience with them. I felt the compassion in my heart. And this was possible because I love myself so much that I do not require their love. Although I am grateful that they clearly cared enough to pick me up from the airport and help support me in various ways throughout the years.

In the car, my mom chatted excitedly with me. I was exhausted after traveling for a full day, and although it was past midnight, my mom wanted to talk during the entire ride. My dad was silent during most of the ride, but I could *feel* his energy. I could feel that he wanted to ask me about my book and didn't know what to say. He knew I was writing it.

A few days after arriving in North Dakota, I finally returned to my roots at my family's farm. The morning of the ritual, I gathered my hapé (sacred tobacco snuff from the Indigenous people of the Amazon), a couple of flashlights, and a cup of coffee, and I drove from my parents' house at 5:00 am to pick up my sister. Sophie brought with her three fruits: an orange, a tangerine, and a pear.

As I waited for Sophie to get into the car, the birds were chirping as though they were excited and knew what we were about to do. The horizon was already beginning to light up with the pale blue of dawn. We drove in excited anticipation, Sophie with her mug of water, and me with my mug of coffee.

I followed a large truck out of town that lurched forward slowly away from the grain elevator. As we continued out of town and down the flat highway, we could see hundreds of miles across the horizon. The prairie opened to us like a book left open to receive the sky. We made our way around the grain truck and headed down the two-lane highway.

Shortly after we left town, we turned onto the familiar gravel road that led to our childhood home. We traveled past a single mobile home, several miles further down the gravel road, past our old mailbox, and down a hill that dropped away to a view of the farm. I felt as though it wasn't only the Native American spirits waiting for us; I felt as though the earth waited for us.

We turned onto the quarter-mile-long driveway situated between two fields that are sometimes filled with corn, sunflowers, oats, or durum—one kind of crop on each side. We continued past the trees that surrounded the Vander Voot homestead, around the curve of the driveway to the east, and parked the blue SUV near a grain bin.

I looked over at Sophie and asked, "Are you ready?"

She nodded.

At first, we walked through the tall grass until we were nearly up to our waists in the prairie grass. Then, as we surveyed the land for the best spot to perform the ritual, we saw an open area next to a corn field. The corn stalks were young in the late spring.

Sophie and I made our way to the clearing, and I found a flat, pink rock that seemed to be the appropriate place to create a makeshift altar. We sat on the ground, looked around at the trees and grass swaying in the wind, and took a deep breath. Sophie handed me the fruit she had brought with her. I immediately began to peel the orange and the tangerine, arranging the pieces in a circle around the pink rock. On top of the rock, I placed the pear.

Then, as I took out my hapé and thanked the Indigenous peoples of the Amazon for allowing me to have this sacred tobacco, I noticed a deer playing nearby. I felt goosebumps as I sprinkled some of the tobacco onto the fruit in reverence.

I began to play "The Message – Tribal Energy Activation" by Matthew Jaidev Duplessie on my cell phone through the app Insight Timer. The wind blew through our hair as we closed our eyes and placed our hands on the earth. This beautiful song made my heart soar each time I heard it and increased my reverent connection to all that is. I sang softly.

After the song ended, I said a prayer and then led Sophie in guided meditation. All of this was done as my intuition led me to do it. "Great Spirit. Divine Goddess. Thank you for being here with us. Thank you for this place, the land where we were raised. We call upon the angelic realm and our Spirit Guides to be with us now. We ask that only love and light enter into our circle. We thank the darkness for our lessons but allow only love and light to be with us now." I could feel we were not alone.

I continued, "We acknowledge the immense suffering that has happened on this earth. We acknowledge the suffering of the Native Americans who were here before our white ancestors who caused their suffering. We know that we cannot change the suffering, but we ask for healing to be upon this place. We ask for healing to touch the past, present, and future. To heal all families that lived here. We recognize the immense loss that happened in this place. And with great respect to the Indigenous Hawaiian people, we repeat their Ho'oponopono prayer to bring love and healing. 'I love you. I'm sorry. Please forgive me. Thank you.'"

After moments of stillness and reverent thanks, I opened my eyes to behold a second deer. I exclaimed, "Sophie, look! Another deer!" We both watched as the deer looked back at us. The deer watched us for a while, then headed toward the trees surrounding the farmhouse. I looked across the prairie illuminated with the sunrise, then back at the deer. One of the deer stood in the light, and one stood in the dark. I stared at the deer, knowing that these deer had been brought to us as a sign. Sophie said to me softly, "Thank you for sharing your gifts."

The sky was alive with a myriad of pinks and oranges as the sun rose on the land. The air around us felt lighter, as though a weight had been lifted from the earth. As I stood to end the ritual, I played the opening of "The Message" song again. I looked down and saw that where I had been sitting was a piece of black rock-like material in the shape of a heart. I picked it up and stared at it because I almost didn't believe what I was seeing.

After we had expressed our thanks to the earth and the spirits there one last time, Sophie and I looked over at a garage with the name of the farm on it. Right above the garage, the new sun was bursting forth, joyfully announcing the new day. I couldn't help but feel that this was the beginning of deep healing for my family and the families of those before us. This was a new dawn.

AKNOWLEDGMENTS

To my husband, for your unwavering support, even when we weren't sure if we could pay for this dream of mine. Thank you for reminding me that it always works out in the end. I love you. Strong together!

To my kids (bio and step), for taking all of those family photos over the years, even when you didn't want to. I love you so much.

To my sisters, colleagues, and friends, who gave me priceless feedback and testimonials. I am so grateful for you.

To the many people who donated to my GoFundMe to make this dream a reality, YOU inspire me to never give up. Sending you so much love for making my dream of becoming a published author come true!

To all my colleagues at an international non-profit who came to my Morning Meditation on Thursdays. I am so grateful I could share guided meditation with you. Whenever I felt overwhelmed, I knew I could count on meditating with you to come back to peace.

To my editors, Gail and Nancy, and my proofreader, Chloë. Thank you for helping me raise my book baby with such care and devotion!

To my publishing team, Bailly and Jenn, at Publish Your Purpose Press. Thank you for helping me feel like a rockstar every step of the way.

To Nelly, for helping me design a stunning book cover.

With great thanks to June Pearl Photography, for the image on the cover of this book! Your work is beautiful, Dorota.

To Mike at Strings & Things Music, for supplying a microphone for my cover photoshoot. You and Judy are some of the best people I know!

To Jen and Vinx, for creating the Vocal Shire Summit where I met fellow incredible singers. You're extraordinary! Amusez-vous bien en France!

To all spiritual healers listed in this book, I am honored to know you: Carlos, Iman, Jeanita, Kim, Amy, and Samantha.

And to you, the reader. Thank you for buying my book. You are so appreciated and loved. May you give yourself grace during your healing journey.

APPENDIX

LEGATO

Legato: *to connect each note smoothly without much articulation between notes*

LGBTQ+ RESOURCES

- Family Equality, www.familyequality.org
  - ○ *Vision statement:*
    - ▪ We envision a future where all LGBTQ families, regardless of creation or composition, live in communities that recognize, respect, protect, and value them.
    - ▪ We envision a world in which every LGBTQ person has the right and the opportunity to form and sustain a loving family, regardless of sexual orientation, gender identity, race, religion, national origin, geography, socioeconomic status, disability, or the intersection of those characteristics.

- Finally, we envision systems of service and support that are free of discrimination and that maximize opportunities for LGBTQ youth needing permanency and LGBTQ adults seeking family formation through adoption, foster care, assisted reproductive technology or other means.
- Gays and Lesbians Against Defamation (GLAAD), www.glaad.org
- Human Rights Campaign (HRC), www.hrc.org
- Lesbian, Gay, Bisexual, and Transgender (LGBT) Hotline: 1-888-843-4564
- Parents, Families, and Friends of Lesbians and Gays, Inc. (PFLAG), www.pflag.org
- Seacoast Outright, *Advocacy and support of LGBTQ+ youth in the Seacoast, New Hampshire*, www.seacoastoutright.com

MENTAL HEALTH RESOURCES

- *Becoming the Narcissist's Nightmare: How to Devalue and Discard the Narcissist While Supplying Yourself* by Shahida Arabi
- *Boundary Boss: The Essential Guide to Talk True, Be Seen, and (Finally) Live Free* by Terri Cole
- *Disarming the Narcissist: Surviving and Thriving with the Self-Absorbed* by Wendy T. Behary
- National Alliance on Mental Illness, www.nami.org
- National Suicide Prevention Lifeline: 1-800-273-8255
- *Power and Control Wheel* from the National Center on Domestic and Sexual Violence
- *Recovery of Your Inner Child* by Lucia Capacchione, Ph.D.

RECOMMENDED SPIRITUAL THOUGHT LEADERS

Amy Major, International Spirit Rescue Specialist, www.amymajor.com

Carlos A. Perez, D.C., Sound Healer, Holistic Chiropractor, and Shaman, www.backinmotionpllc.com

Iman Gatti, Grief Recovery Specialist and Life Coach, www.imangatti.com

Jeanita Kennedy of the Diné (Navajo) Nation, Healer of Healers and Photographer, https://jkennedyservice.zenfolio.com/rswelcome

Kim LaJoie, Integrated Awareness, https://www.alignable.com/concord-nh/integrated-awarenesd

Rachel Merrill, Reiki Master and Holistic Life Coach, www.rachelmerrill.me

Samantha Shea, Holistic Life Coach, Regression Hypnotherapy, Trance Healer, www.branchesofvibrationalhealing.com

STEPMOM RESOURCES

The Happy Stepmother by Rachelle Katz

Say Goodbye to Crazy: How to Rid Yourself of that Crazy Ex and Restore Sanity to Your Life by Dr. Tara Palmatier and Paul Elam

The Smart Stepmom: Practical Steps to Help You Thrive by Ron L. Deal and Laura Petherbridge

Will I Ever Be Good Enough? Healing the Daughters of Narcissistic Mothers by Karyl McBride, Ph.D.

SPIRITUAL RESOURCES

All books by Thich Nhat Hanh

Ask and It Is Given by Esther and Jerry Hicks

Cracked Open – Never Broken: A Memoir by Iman Gatti

Plan It by the Planets The AstroTwins, https://astrostyle.com/

Finally Full of Yourself: Unlocking Your Spiritual DNA by Maria Salomão-Schmidt

Healing with the Angels by Doreen Virtue, Ph.D.

The Healing Power of the Human Voice: Mantras, Chants, and Seed Sounds for Health and Harmony by James D'Angelo

The Healing Power of Witchcraft by Meg Rosenbriar

The Healing Wisdom of Africa by Malidoma Patrice Somé

Judgement Detox by Gabrielle Bernstein

Letters to a Starseed by Rebecca Campbell

Light is the New Black by Rebecca Campbell

May Cause Miracles by Gabrielle Bernstein
The Shaman's Toolkit by Sandra Ingerman
Spellwork for Self-Care: 40 Spells to Soothe the Spirit by Lyn Pastuhova
The World of Shamanism by Roger Walsh, M.D., Ph.D.
You are Magical by Tess Whitehurst

OTHER RESOURCES

American-Arab Anti-Discrimination Committee https://www.adc.org/
National Association for the Advancement of Colored People (NAACP)
     https://naacp.org/
Standing Rock Reservation https://www.standingrock.org/

ABOUT THE AUTHOR

Rachel Merrill, author of *I Sang Anyway: A Stepmom's Spiritual Memoir of Healing*, is passionate about human potential. She grew up on a farm in North Dakota, USA, and moved to Vermont for graduate school in 2006. Rachel spent more than a decade fighting poverty and hunger in New Hampshire as a manager for the welfare to work program for single parents.

Some of her specialized knowledge includes French, Indigenous Rights, the topics of mental health, substance misuse, domestic violence, and workforce development. In addition, she is a certified Diversity & Cultural Competence trainer. She has enjoyed working in refugee resettlement, as a camp counselor for kids from inner-city Chicago, and as a grant writer for Life & Water Development – Cameroon, among other jobs. Rachel has worked for an international non-profit since December 2018 where she leads guided meditation for their employees. She is a fundraiser inspiring giving from individual donors and community groups. She holds a Master's in Social Justice in Intercultural Relations from the School for International Training (SIT) Graduate Institute.

Rachel is a Reiki Master, Certified Holistic Life Coach, witch, singer, writer, wife, mom, and stepmom. To learn more about working with Rachel, or to inquire about a speaking engagement, please visit www.RachelMerrill.me.

DOWNLOAD YOUR FREE HEALING MEDITATION

To download your free Healing Meditation,
visit www.rachelmerrill.me/meditation.

CPSIA information can be obtained
at www.ICGtesting.com
Printed in the USA
BVHW041121301221
625197BV00018B/720/J